D0828764

MAVERICK WESTERN VERSE

MAVERICK
WESTERN VERSE

Edited by
John C. Dofflemyer

GIBBS·SMITH
P
PUBLISHER

First Edition

96 95 94   10 9 8 7 6 5 4 3 2 1

Introduction copyright © 1994 by John Dofflemyer

Poetry copyrights remain property of individual poets.

All rights reserved. No part of this publication may be
reproduced or transmitted in any form or by any means,
electronic or mechanical, without written permission
from the publisher.

This is a Peregrine Smith Book, published by
Gibbs Smith, Publisher
P.O. Box 667
Layton, Utah 84041

Book design by J. Scott Knudsen, Park City, Utah
Cover art: *Bring in the Strays* by Howard Post
Lynda Sessions, Editor
Dawn Valentine Hadlock, Editorial Assistant

Interior illustrations on the title page, pages 19, 25, 39,
77, 93, 104 and 109 by Will James from *Cowboys North
and South*, published by Grosset & Dunlap, 1924
Interior illustrations on pages 28, 131 and 151 by Will
James from *Cow Country*, published by Grosset &
Dunlap, 1927 Interior illustrations on pages xii, 33, 53,
55, 59, 103, 161 and 165 by Will James from *All in the
Day's Riding*, published by Charles Scribner's Sons, 1943
Interior illustrations on pages 21, 27, 97, 137, 139 and
141 by Herman Palmer from *Hidden Heroes of the
Rockies*, published by World Book Company, 1923
Interior illustration on page 62, by Carl Eytel from the
book *The Wonders of the Colorado Desert*, published by
Boston Little, Brown, and Company, 1906

Printed and bound in the United States of America

ISBN 0-87905-594-4 (pbk.)

to Maverick Western Verse

The first Cowboy Poetry Gathering in Elko, Nevada in 1985 has become a landmark in time and place for in the years since, contemporary cowboy expression has exploded into 150 similar gatherings annually across the Western United States that establish cowboy poetry as an increasingly popular phenomenon not only offering entertainment, but also marketing hundreds of volumes of poetry in numbers heretofore unmatched by any other genre of poetry. The first Cowboy Poetry Gathering was sprung as the modest brainchild of, among others, folklorist, Hal Cannon and poet, Waddie Mitchell, to celebrate the classic cowboy oral tradition. One must marvel at how it has evolved in ten short years.

Perhaps the most neglected aspect of this phenomenon in its significance to cowboy poets is that this geographically scattered and isolated livelihood has been reunited. Poetically silent for nearly fifty years since the classic, Kiplingesque laments of a dying breed which signified the imminent changes facing the cowboy, most, including today's cowboys and ranchers, considered the culture all but dead. Now often likened to family reunions, Elko and subsequent gatherings have fortified this growing number of writers in a contagious atmosphere of acceptance born out of a common livelihood. This livelihood has always been tied to the intriguing whims of nature while being bombarded on a myriad of fronts by the demands of encroaching progress. It is here at these gatherings that poets draw strength from one another, share gossip, news and problems, with, and in addition to, the unabashed perspectives of their poetry. For many, Elko has become the heart of the culture, an annual trek for rejuvenation, an epiphany. In practice, it has established an interdependent sense of rural community on a larger scale, as most poets now network vis à vis the mail, telephone or with an occasional fax machine between the few gatherings that time and work allows them to attend. Almost out of deprivation, this renewed grassroots voice has quickly evolved in many diverse directions.

Simplistically, the mythological, past tense hyperbole in the classic oral tradition is now giving way to a more imperative, present tense urgency in both form and content. Maverick Western Verse is intended to incorporate the diverse shape of this evolution since its resurgence. It is also intended to broaden our conception of this expression with the inclusion of some poetry coincidentally written without the spiritual benefits of Elko, yet rooted in this same livestock culture. With as many as six other anthologies currently in the works at this time, this is not an all-inclusive collection of contemporary cowboy poetry, but rather offers poetry which has taken risks within the genre, which dares new subject matter, which offers insight on more contemporary levels of humanness unattended by more postured collections, seeking - and I sense always seeking - an oral quality consistent with the culture and each individual poet. These are the mavericks, the individualists, the remnants of a pioneering breed dealing with a modern age of fast and changing values.

That both the content and form from these poets is diverse, encompassing even the most contemporary issues, is not surprising. As Western verse evolves with the culture while extremely aware of environmental and social issues in that process, a unique blend of realities occurs. Rural communities still judge men and women by what they can do, neighbors know and depend upon one another, reputations and identities are constantly updated and ultimately weighed in terms of the community's well-being. From a lifestyle with few secrets, it is this honesty and that interdependence of self-reliant rural individuals I hope to bring to this anthology. That the amazing evolution of contemporary cowboy poetry follows this same rural blueprint may demonstrate why "cowboy individualism" is not a threat to the community, but it is that very trait which unites one to the other with a practical sense of usefulness, and perhaps the rural culture, like the poetry, may yet flourish with a renewed interest and understanding of the land and its people.

If poetry matters, if it serves a function, it makes perfect sense that it should come from a culture with "hands-on" experience. Whether this function may only be anecdotal wisdom gleaned from trails already traveled, therapeutically or otherwise, or whether it may offer survival facts, tools or templates, or insightful meanderings across a well-known landscape, or merely an attempt to bridge that rural/urban gap, it balances art with instrument. It is this balance which has evolved from an oral, storytelling heritage to something hopefully more timely and useful.

John Dofflemyer

In attempting to keep consistent this powerful individualism, I may have tarnished the untouchable, Hollywood icon of the American cowboy as being human and more identifiably real. As values and traditions gained from our upbringings are constantly confronted with majority politics and theoretical philosophies, we struggle to adapt, knowing first hand from our natural environment, the consequence of failing, yet we depend on experience and the experience of generations which has survived with us. The adaptation process is never easy and the sorting requires an open and introspective mind as this everpresent contrast of realities screams to be addressed.

The revitalization of this oral tradition attracts both rural and urban audiences, often numbering in excess of ten thousand at Elko, to celebrate and communicate an alternative, but basic lifestyle. But this rural sense of tribe, however, differs from most urban concepts of community which have become increasingly dependent upon rules and regulations for conformity. Interestingly, this difference sticks in the craws of both cultures, resulting in a distinct sense of distrust, each of the other.

My involvement with cowboy poetry as both a poet and editor of Dry Crik Review, has always been to bridge that rural/urban chasm with communication. As my generational roots run deeply within this rural culture, I hope to bring a more personal perspective to this anthology from the inside-out, rather than with the scrutiny of an outsider looking to identify quaint foibles, rituals or cultural consistencies as if we, the evolving offspring, live and work on a microscopic slide. Hopefully, this perspective is of value to both communities. We are, like everyone else, a hybrid product of the times, but crossed with an unusual proportion of independence in our poetry as in our lives.

Elizabeth Bancroft, "Winter Solstice" was first published in *Dry Crik Review.*

C. J. Berkman, "In The Blood" from *In The Blood,* Saddle Tramp Publications, 1992.

Doris Bircham, "he tells it like it was" was first published in *Riding the Northern Range, Poems of the Last Best-West,* Red Deer College Press, 1993.

Ed Brown, "In The Eye Of The Beholder" was first published in *Dry Crik Review.*

Laurie Wagner Buyer, "The Smell Of Sage" was first published in *Dry Crik Review.*

Ron Chappell, "Kings, Tonight" and "Cliff Dwellers" were first published in *Dry Crik Review.*

Ruth Daniels, "Small Town Dying" and "Noise Level" were first published in *Dry Crik Review.*

Jay Dusard, "Southwestern Suite," "Good Buckskin Horse" and "Spring, 1965" were first published in *Dry Crik Review.*

Jon Forrest Glade, "Route 138" was first published in *Dry Crik Review.*

Jim Green, "Branding Day" was first published in *CV II* and *White Clouds Revue, #2.* "Mountain Likker" was first published in *Grain.* "Hired Guns" and "Bounty Hunter" were first published in *Dry Crik Review.* "Hired Guns" is also included in *Riding the Northern Range, Poems of the Last Best-West,* Red Deer College Press, 1993.

Jim Hammons, "Practicality" was first published in *Dry Crik Review.*

Cynthia J. Harper, "Shipwreck, New Mexico" was first published in *Dry Crik Review.*

Linda Hasselstrom, "Uncle" was first published in *Prairie Winds*, Spring, 1992. "Spring" was first published in *South Dakota Review*, in Summer, 1978. "Digging Potatoes" was first published in *Passages North* in August, 1990. All three are included in *Dakota Bones*, Spoon River Poetry Press, 1993. "Drought Year" was first published in *Nebraska Territory* in 1991 and is included in *Land Circle, Writings Collected from the Land*, Fulcrum Publishing, 1991.

Bill Jones, "American Hero" from *Blood Trails*, Dry Crik Press, 1992. "The Luck Of The Draw" was first published in *Dry Crik Review*.

Teresa Jordan, "Old Anne" was first published in *Northern Lights* and *Dry Crik Review*. "Looking Back" was first published in *Poetry Flash* and from *Riding the White Horse Home*, Pantheon Books, 1993.

Greg Keeler, "Llamas In The Landscape," was first published in *Montana Sketchbook*, 1989 by the Montana Institute of the Arts, "Do Not Ask" was first published in *Plains Poetry Journal*, and both included in *Epiphany at Goofy's Gas*, Clark City Press, 1991. "What's Left of the West" was first published in *Late Harvest*, Paragon House Publishers, 1991. "Coyote's Wilderness Lobby" from *All You Can Eat*, Rampant Rat Productions, 1992.

Mike Logan, "Temptation" was first published in *The Montana Stockgrower* and is included in *Laugh Kills Lonesome*, Buglin' Bull Press, 1991.

Jo-Ann Mapson, "Rock Solid Women," "Time Before Winter," "Poor Man's Silver," and "Notes On Aging" all appear in the chapbook *Spooking The Horses*, Thunder and Thistle Press, 1991.

Rod McQueary, "Work for Food" was first published in *Dry Crik Review*, "for souls" was first published in *Dry Crik Review* and from *Blood Trails*, Dry Crik Press, 1992, and appeared in *Coolin' Down, An Anthology of Contemporary Cowboy*

Poetry, Guy Logsdon Books, 1992.

Larry McWhorter, "The Panhandle" was first published in *Dry Crik Review.*

Neil Meili, "Memories of three or four" was first published in *Dry Crik Review.* "The Lonely Men" was first published in *Riding the Northern Range, Poems from the Last Best-West,* Red Deer College Press, 1993.

Wayne Nelson, "The Lesson" was first published in *Dry Crik Review.*

Jennifer Olds, "Culling The Herd" was first published by *Staple Magazine,* Yorkshire, England and "The Murder of Crows" was first published in the chapbook, *Half-Acre Ranch,* First Edition Press, 1992.

Barbara Shirk Parrish, "Reasons for Rain," "Night Legacy" and "Grandmother's Land" were first published in *Dry Crik Review.*

Shadd Piehl, "Storm Front," "Papa Sapa," "My Grandfather's and Father's Horses," and "Riding Song" were first published in *Dry Crik Review.* "Towards Horses" was first published in *Aluminum Canoe.*

Charles Potts, "Uncle Tom's Sawmill," "Starlight On The Trail," "Cowboys Between Ranches," "A Monkey In The High 90's" and "Make Way For Daniel Boone" were first published in *Dry Crik Review.*

Lisa Quinlan, "Escape" was first published in *Dry Crik Review.*

Vess Quinlan, "St Francis 1951" and "Coyotes and Watermelons" from *The Trouble With Dreams,* Wind Vein Press, 1990. "The Trophy" was first published in *Dry Crik Review.*

Jim "Tex" Raths, "John Deere Dreaming" was first published in *Dry Crik Review.*

Buck Ramsey, "Poem Notes" was first published in *Dry Crik Review.*

Hank Real Bird, "Lone Star Woman" and "Driftwood Feelin'" were first published in *Where Shadows are Born*, in 1990 and were reprinted by the University of Findlay in 1992.

"Kell Robertson, "The Old Man Goes Home" was first published in *Dry Crik Review*. "Green Lantern Bar/El Paso, Texas" from *Bear Crossing*, Guerilla Poetics Books, 1989.

Anne Slade, "lawrence" and "farmers still" have been aired by CBC.

Myrt Wallis, "Love And War" was first published in *Dry Crik Review*.

Sue Wallis, "Grandpa Lew," first published in *Dry Crik Review*, "Coyote Bitch," first published in *Poetry Flash*, and "Girlfriends" all from *The Exalted One*, Dry Crik Press, 1991.

Andy Wilkinson, "At the Grave of Billy the Kid," "Horseback on the Llano Estacado," and "F.M. 168, Buffalo Lake to Nazareth" were first published in *Dry Crik Review*.

Keith Wilson, "Portrait of a Father," "Spring," and "Cow Dogs" were first published in *Kayak*. "The People from the Valley" was first published in *Bluefish*. "Desert Cenote" was first published by *Great Raven Press*, 1971.

William Wood, "Fleeting Moments" was first published in *Dry Crik Review*.

Jerry Wright, "The Four Horse Hitch" was first published in *Dry Crik Review*.

Paul Zarzyski, "Flamenca Duende" was first published in a limited edition chapbook *The Garnet Moon*, University of Nevada Press, Reno, 1990 and republished with "Maria Benitez" as a broadsheet by Wind Vein Press, and included in *White Clouds Revue*, #5. "Zarzyski Stomachs the Oxford Special With Zimmer at the Ox Bar & Grill" was first published in *Roughstock Sonnets* by The Lowell Press, 1989.

LAWN LESSONS

Elizabeth Bancroft

Lord, how we laughed
when dogs got connected!
Grownups hated it.
Stuck-together yelping dogs
sunburned adult faces &
stiffened them so they
couldn't laugh, but their
old eyes looked every which
way except on each others'
so they wouldn't slip a
chuckle, then one'd say,
"git 'n the house" to us.
Somebody always turned on
the hose, or sloshed a bucket
of water, & we couldn't figure
why they thought being wet
would matter to those dogs.

WINTER SOLSTICE

ELIZABETH BANCROFT

Work horses, eyes closed
hair winter length
falsely fluffy
tailed the wind for warmth.
He hailed them over the gate,
cracked ice in their trough.
They stood hard.

As if their hooves would
fracture frozen clods
their muscles hunched
strained hulky bodies
to be light
gingerly stepping
as he led them to the barn.

I hated the days horses
left their pastures
for dry hay & immovable
heat from coal stoves.
Fall done, life became
bundled, familiar objects
fumbled under gloves.
Winter permitted no
human grace
movements ice-slip,
tight gaited—or dash
from place to place.

The trees no longer hid
hills ranging distant.
Vision was magnified
air crystalled so clear
the foreign & the known
took new perspective;
everything was single
encased by cold. Even
telephone wires were lonely
without birds.

IN THE BLOOD

C. J. BERKMAN

I'm Indian.
I know I don't look it,
but one-eighth of the blood
which pumps through me
is Choctaw blood.
I never thought about it
until recently.
Going through
some old family photographs,
an old picture of John Thorn—
my mother's grandfather—surfaced.
He stared back at me,
all defiant in his buckskins,
high-topped boots,
braids hanging over both shoulders.
I looked into his eyes,
saw my own reflection . . .

My mother
never mentioned
her grandfather to me,
didn't want to talk about
this Choctaw ancestor
who left Oklahoma in 1876
to make a fortune
milling Louisiana pine.

My grandmother—his daughter—
told me stories about him
when my mother wasn't around,
stories about how he'd left
the reservation in Oklahoma
with his racing horse,
made enough money
with that horse
to settle down
around Gueydan,
marry my great-grandmother
against her father's wishes,
made them a good living
with his lumbermill.
Then one day a man
named Dupree accused
John Thorn
of cheating him
over a stand of timber.

My grandmother
told me of the night
Dupree and his sons
burned the mill,
the lumberyard,
to the ground.
The next day
Dupree's sons

were bragging
about how
they'd taught
the Indian
how White Men
did their business.
John Thorn's brother-in-law,
Jesse Doucet,
warned John Thorn
that he should stay
out of Gueydan
that day, let the high sheriff
handle this business.
John Thorn picked up
his shotgun,
a pocket full of shells,
saddled his racing horse,
went into town.

He found Dupree
and his two sons
in a poolroom downtown.
Dupree drew his pistol first,
but when it was over,
Dupree and his oldest son
were dead or dying
on the pool room floor.
John Thorn, the Choctaw Indian,
walked away without a scratch.

He mounted his racing horse,
rode back home
to await the high sheriff
and his deputies.

The high sheriff came,
took John Thorn to jail.
There was a trial,
but Dupree's youngest son
admitted that his father
had burned the mill,
had drawn his pistol
when he saw John Thorn
enter the poolroom.

John Thorn never rebuilt
his sawmill, lumberyard.
He took my great-grandmother
and moved to Texas,
began farming 600 acres
around Gonzales.
My grandmother said
for the rest of his life,
he never mentioned Louisiana.

My mother never told anyone
that she had Choctaw blood,
or that her grandfather had killed

two men in Louisiana.
I can recall my father
teasing my mother about
her wild Indian blood.
She never once laughed.

When I was older,
I was a wild child.
My father's father
said it was just
My Injun blood.
My mother never laughed
at that, either.
I think that when
she looked at me,
she saw the eyes
of that old Choctaw killer
staring back at her
just as defiant as
the old photograph
she kept with
her mother's things
in an old trunk
in a corner
of the attic . . .

he tells it like it was

DORIS BIRCHAM

over thirty years I bin ranchin' an' I ain't seen
nothin' like it before just out ridin' checkin' my herd
one evenin' when I sees this cow tryin' to calve an'
a mean ol' cow she is too an' I see the tips of the
calf's feet showin' an' wouldn't you know there's
two hind feet you can tell the hind ones 'cause
they're upside down but that cow settles right in to
pushin' has that calf all by herself even though it's
comin' backwards she jumps right up starts mooin'
and lickin' an' I'm some relieved so I rides off a
hundred yards or so where another cow's gettin'
right to it I look 'er over the water bag's just
startin' to show she'll be awhile yet and when I
rides back to that first cow there she is lyin' flat
out an' I say sure as hell she must be havin' twins
but no she's deader 'n road kill stretched out on
that hillside with a chunk of the calf bag hangin'
out her mouth you know that slimy skin the calf's
born in not the afterbirth hell no just the calf bag so
I jumps off my horse I pull on that skin but it breaks
right off couldn't have done a damn thing if I'd
been right there while she was chokin' the calf's
standin' there beside its dead mother just standin'
lookin' up at me so I heads for home gets me a
bottle an' I milk that dead cow pour that first milk
into the calf seems like the best thing I can do for
the both of them for now with it so close to bein'
dark

TRANSPLANTED

DORIS BIRCHAM

he takes 63's calf
when he thinks she's not looking
drags it from the pen
quietly closes the metal gate
      tells his son
he's kept the old cow
one year too long
her breathing's gone bad
now she's turned up lame

he skins the stillborn calf
born an hour ago to a 3-year-old heifer
places the stillborn's hide like a jacket
over the calf he stole
from old 63
      he watches
as the heifer and calf mother up
says the old cow will get a chance
to fatten up now
      before he sells her
and the calf will have a mother
who gives enough milk
old 63 bawls only occasionally
he tries not to look her way
when he rides past her pen
yet even when he's at the far end
of the pasture
      and his back is turned
he feels her gaze
steady upon him

MORNING PRELUDE

Doris Bircham

though sunrise haze I watch
twenty—two blue herons
land at the edge
of the stubble, stand
motionless as if not knowing
what to do when away
from water and sky

poplar leaves dance
to a background breeze
while frogs strum their chords
in a nearby slough

in soft diminuendos
the herons lift from the field
their long necks folded
dagger beaks extended
legs trail far behind
huge wings stroke
the air, the blue-grey
sweep of feathers binding
me and the clouds
to the music of morning

CENTENNIAL QUILTING

Doris Bircham

Her hands shake a little
as she holds needle and thread
to the light. Blue veins
outline the wear of a century.
She weaves back and forth, follows
each log cabin stitch, remembers
another cabin, an old washtub
squatted on her black cookstove,
flames snapping and the smell
of fresh bread in every corner.

The stitches are red, they could be
jars of tomatoes lined on a sideboard,
apples bending branches
outside her back door,
small polka dots on the scarf
she wears to church.

She looks past a geranium
to vegetable rows outside her window
then turns, glances at the picture
taken on her birthday
where a small woman sits straight
behind candles and flowers.
I don't feel that old. She adjusts
her quilting frame, continues stitching

in rows, feels the pull of afternoon sun
the roughness of a hoe handle
inside her palm.

When it's time to rest
she makes a pot of tea, pours
until her cup is full. She recalls
old friends, one by one, now gone.
Their troubles all started
when they stopped doing things.
You have to keep doing things
in the evening light
with hands that move back and forth
stitching both sides
of the fabric together.

IN THE EYE OF THE BEHOLDER

ED BROWN

"Of course I'll come," I answered,
When I got the foreman's call.
I like to help the neighbors when I can.
My irrigation water wouldn't
Miss me much at all,
And there's not a better thing to do than brand.

Bright and early the next morning,
I went quickly out the door,
As the little stars were starting to go out
And I rattled 'cross the cattle guard
Contented to the core,
'Cuz brandings are what this life's all about.

Though I didn't know this outfit,
I'd know most the fellers there.
The ranching world is really kind of small.
Then I had no way of knowing
When the ropers were all paired,
I'd be roping with the master of them all.

He was clearly pushing eighty
When we all shook hands around.
Never met before but I sure knew his name.
And before the day was over
I was certain that I'd found
Several pieces of this puzzling living game.

Swinging overhand reata,
Reg'lar as a metronome,
On a black colt poised and ready every beat,
He would sail it towards the target
And it always found a home
On an unsuspecting calf's head or two feet.

Not an ounce of wasted energy,
The big black colt moved out
In a confident, slow way that I admired.
Never hurried, never hustled,
We just turned each horse about
And another calf was stretched right by the fire.

When we broke for lunch I noted
On his colt tied by the fence
With the faded saddle fenders in the sun,
that he'd won it as a trophy
In a bridle horse event.
It said, "Santa Barbara, 1941."

I admired it for its beauty,
Nearly hidden by its age.
It was finely crafted, rigging to the horn.
Every scar on it was history.
I could read it page by page,
And he'd won it seven years 'fore I was born.

As the branding was concluded,
One young roper that I'd met,
Who'd been running his poor pony from the start,
Gave his horse one final jerking,
Covered up with foam and sweat,
Up and asked me, "Where'd you dig up this old fart?"

Every nerve I have said, "Hit him!"
But instead I let it pass.
His arena broke ideas are common stuff.
His mind was wrapped with inner tube.
Equating 'good' with 'fast'.
I think ignorance is punishment enough.

MUD CREEK BEAVER

Laurie Wagner Buyer

Little worker I've walked a mile in these hot, floppy
irrigation boots to undo what you spent all night doing.

At dawn the water is not on the fields as it should be.
Of course you're the culprit, creator of deep ponds.

I search for you upstream, but now that your work is
done, you've gone under, hidden away from the sun.

Sighing, I slide down the steep bank into black water.
All night you cut willows, dabbed mud, built this dam.

Intricate and entwined, hard to dismantle, I spend hours
pulling each stick carefully, reversing your pattern.

Once I saw you sitting upright in the grass, balanced
by your broad tail, cleaning your rusty, oil-slick fur.

I caught you listening, stopped by some strange sound,
a half-chewed willow branch between your artistic paws.

At dusk I return, see you swimming circles in rosy light,
the whacking slap of your flat tail a wondrous warning.

I raise my rifle slowly, so very cold and heavy,
so uncompromising in my trembling, hesitant hands.

THROUGH ASPENS AND BEYOND

LAURIE WAGNER BUYER

Our woodstove blazes against winter.
Still the cold seeps in with silence.

Circling with wary snarls, this vicious
war worries us, frays us apart.

Years and years of sparring, skirmishes,
testing your strength against my weakness,

your right against my wrong—they say
knowing the enemy is half the battle—

but after all this precious time I know
nothing of your head, your heart, your cause;

I've only memorized the lean line of
your groin, the tight set of your jaw.

Our paths diverge. You forge through
pines to fight darkness encroaching;

I bend toward the light,
through aspens and beyond.

SMELL OF SAGE

Laurie Wagner Buyer

Autumns ago we rode bareback for sage,
crossing and re-crossing river channels,
urging our mounts through ancient sloughs,
brush-choked islands. We talked then,
sometimes sang, passing the miles with
laughter until reaching the vista:

Sage creek pouring out of Canada,
long bars of pebbled sand, and above,
a bluff so high we craned our necks
to see a wizened pine on top. The horses
tugged their bits, wanting to run;
we whooped and shouted, plunged 'cross
the creek mouth and down the smooth
bars; sun and spray dazzling our eyes
until the horses lost all footing and
swam, wide-eyed and snorting for the high bank.

The lone pine wore our dripping clothes,
your buckskins and moccasins, my socks and jeans—
the clash of cultures hanging in a tree—still,
stringing us together, our vision of mated
redtails circling the sky and the drifting
smell of sage.

Toweled by the wind, we descended, the horses
haunch-sliding their way down rocky deer
trails. The flat was endless; a prehistoric
riverbed, aspen-ringed, where now sagebrush grew.
Leaving the horses to trail their reins, we knelt,
snipped silver-green leaves into a leather pouch,
the herb to spice our sausage and stew, the pungent
odor filling our afternoon.

This autumn, returning to your world, I thought
that time lost to us. But, mid-winter, unknowing,
a visiting friend brought with her a sprig of sage.
By lamplight, watching you stitch a deer skin, she
unbraided and brushed my tangled hair. The smell
of sage reached us, seeping through our differences,
tying a loose, but lasting, common bond.

HAIKU FROM THE MOUNTAINS

Laurie Wagner Buyer

Water rush on stone,
coyote calling all alone;
starlight spills on me.

Cattails dance at dawn,
arced arms rising from the slough;
storm skies seem like eyes.

No cows to be found,
lone bull elk bugles again,
paws the leaf strewn ground.

Swollen breast of moon,
nighthawk sinks in summer haze;
breeze brushes my hair.

Skyborne eagle stoops,
shadow striking over me;
the sun disappears.

Behind restless clouds,
winter's bright and full face moon;
the cry of an owl.

Abandoned in flight,
a crow's ebony feather
drifts slowly earthward.

A bony armed tree,
endless acres winter snow;
all seems forgotten.

CLIFF DWELLERS

RON CHAPPELL

Shy, they hover in the shadows
along the broken ledges
still as idols in the twilight
as they contemplate the scene
from their dwellings in the darkness
I almost feel them at the edges
of the hollow doors and windows
as I ford their little stream.

As sunset flings its arrows
in a final parting volley
it illuminates the kivas
to rekindle ancient soul
and the canyon walls re-echo
with the mystery of their folly
once again they come to season
by the magic of its glow.

Slowly darkness cloaks the Mesa
and their scurry's all around me
as my campfire warms the flavor
of the pinyon scented air
and softly through the somber
I sense them reaching, almost touch me
as they shimmer on the fringes
in little shows of ghostly dare

From the broken pots around me
I cull a shard of subtle lining
and an instant silvery laughter
seems to float upon the breeze
while I peer into the darkness
hoping for some secret signing
of the potter as she hides there
in the scatter of the trees

Gone, these thousand years now
in their natural and good order
still they roam the hidden reaches
 . . . archaic margins of my mind
and they call me, seem to know me
from an age beyond some border
where the eons gather stardust
from a people lost in time.

KINGS, TONIGHT

RON CHAPPELL

The stove glows red
in the herders tent,
somewhere . . . just west
of the divide.

Icy pellets,
driven by a nasty wind
slap canvas
. . . make me think of home.

Horse blankets and saddles
make fine couches though,
The herder knows no better
poor folks have poor ways.

What luck, to find this camp
in early winter blizzard that
no man could foresee.
. . . I shiver at the alternative.

"Joaquine" he says, "from Peru"
exhausting his supply of English.
we settle on a bastard Spanish,
. . . his no better than mine.

A leg of lamb hangs by a wire
just above his crackling stove,
dripping savory juices
into a boiling can below.

Just to one side bread
rises in a pan . . . waiting
for the fire to die
    . . . enough to use the oven.

Blackberry brandy
from a saddlebag
is passed back and forth
until we become old friends.

While the wind howls
he tells me of Peru
Laughing softly
over mugs of steaming coffee.

He lifts his head, listens
to ancient murmurings
within the storm, and
knows we have all night.

He takes his time now
the words hanging
like Peruvian Condors
above the Andes.

There's much I need to know,
he thinks
about his village
below Machu Pichu.

He serves the bread and lamb
on tin plates, smiling shyly
he apologizes
for the poorness of the fare.

Secretly, I know
that somewhere tonight,
there are kings
who fare no better.

. . . And I know all
I need to know
about Peru . . .

NOISE LEVEL
Ruth Daniels

I can't endure the city traffic,
ring and blare of bell and horn.
The clattering, hurrying,
bustling.

But . . . I do not hear unless I want
the cacophony of the country air.

Treefrogs, cicadas, the mockingbird,
jeers of the raucous crow,
buzz of bees,
cattle bedding down . . .
the howl of the coyote vies
with the call of the dove.

SMALL TOWN DYING

RUTH DANIELS

Finch's Fine Furniture
now a surplus store;
truckloads of groceries . . .
food stamps taken.
Dee's Diner boarded up,
Dallas bound.

The theatre on the corner of Broadway,
a blind marquee
and gutted hull smell of decay.
The Santa Fe Station
now the Chamber of Commerce
needs a coat of paint . . .
The courthouse clock gave up in '82
only robins busy on the square.

The fancy shoe store's gone.
No more boutiques.
Four empty buildings
on the south side of Main.
two plants have closed . . .
the unemployment lines
wrap 'round the building,
full bars along the block on Reno.

Young men walk old men's steps,
eyes mirror lost hope.
Farmers sell garden sass
from the back of pickup trucks
in the vacant parking lot . . .
Cheap fodder for the forgotten.

SPRING, 1965
JAY DUSARD

The tallow truck winch
draws my buckskin up the ramp.
I hate long goodbyes.

GOOD BUCKSKIN HORSE
JAY DUSARD

Yellow trimmed in black;
hipper than Eohippus.
Cow-huntin' mother.

SOUTHWESTERN SUITE

JAY DUSARD

WINTER

Ice two inches thick
on the horse trough. Brown colt bucks;
great to be alive.

SPRING

Blooming daffodils
ambushed by late April snow
better cowboy-up.

SUMMER

Cumulonimbus
shadows across dry ridges.
Maybe it will rain.

FALL

Roundup circles sweep
golden country. Weaned calves bawl.
Load 'em on the trucks.

ROUTE 138
JON FORREST GLADE

Near St. Stephens Mission
the asphalt is stained
with cheap white wine
and the blood of Arapahoes.

Stumbling in the dark,
looking for an answer, looking
for the happy hunting grounds,
they reach out to headlights.

HIRED GUNS
JIM GREEN

All night long they lay
forted on the bale stack
wrapped in parkas and robes
against the driving snow,
the icy midnight winds.

Waiting with covered guns
eyes knifing the black
and flying flakes
of February winter,
sipping thermos coffee,
wishing they were home.

Finally   the elk came,
gaunt shadows in the blur
they trod cautiously
hooves cracking crust
stopping   listening
     starving   advancing
driven from the mountains
hunger   overcoming fear
   closer
        closer
          then wheeling
   away in terror
racing from gun thunder,
splash of pluming rifles.

Climbing down off the stack
stiff   smell of cordite,
cold   sounds of running
the wind   and tomorrow
more of the same   saving
the hay   for the cattle.

MOUNTAIN LIKKER

JIM GREEN

Usta be powerful likker around,
yu'd hitch up yr team a dogs
head in t town fr the weekend
n haul back yr bran yr rice
n yr sugar all good clean food,
round up a length of copper pipe
run in some cold crick water,
chop a pile a wood fr the fire.

Now there's ways n ways
to test a likker's kick.
Yu cin burn it in a spoon
n if it blazes bright blue
well that's good stuff,
or yu cin take a stiff whiff
n if yr nose turns dead numb
clear down to yr eye teeth
that's drinking moonshine.

But the one truth test
is t toss off half a cup
n if yu cain't hit th ground
with three throws a yr hat,
that there's a man's drink.

I heard tell some time later
that them two ol brothers
would skin a jug of moonshine
out back to the ol log barn
and after polishing it all off
one of'm would crawl on over
to the other side of the stall
and the other brother would
have to make his best guess
as to which one of'm done it.

BOUNTY HUNTER

JIM GREEN

Here's a black and white snapshot
from my high school photo album
showing a grey 1950's Land Rover
with two dead cougars on the hood,
blood dribbling down the fenders
to pool rust red in the gutter,
flow lava like to an iron grate
out front of Graham's Barber Shop.

It doesn't show the cougar killer
who's in the King Edward Hotel
holding court with shots of rye
and beer chasers to a wild crowd
of primed back thumpers who seem
to have their blood up and all
of them at the same time dying
to tell their own time worn tales.

It doesn't show the two hounds
in the back of the bloody Rover.
The old bitch with heaving sides
intestines spilling from her belly
welling out across the cold floor
and it doesn't show the other dog,
the young Black and Tan runner
licking the stump of its left leg,
lungs full of the smell of death,
eyes wide with pain and fear.

BRANDING DAY

JIM GREEN

A reasonable beginning
we started out the day
having a bottle of beer
each time the catch pen was empty
cool bottle from the horse trough
as two riders cut out more calves
but it got hotter   and hotter
as the afternoon wore on
beer came faster and faster
with fewer calves   being a penful
another beer
then a beer every six calves
soon there's a few left
so it's a beer a calf
one calf   one bottle
one catch pen   one calf
one bottle   one catch pen of beer
and after the calves   a rodeo
with two tired horses
till one guy broke his shoulder
another gallops to his aide
vaults from the saddle
breaks his fool leg
and we all get kicked out
of the Cardston hospital
by three flapping
black and white nuns
and an old geezer in a wheelchair
wearing pale blue pyjamas
with the fly wide open.

GOING TO BUY SOME HEIFERS
The Death of Jesse Parker

DRUM HADLEY

We turn onto a dirt road. Calves scamper away
    toward the West, tail hairs flying,
    shimmering in the sunlight.
"I'll bet those little farts 'll weigh 500 pounds
    in the Fall, if it rains," Bill Bryan says.
"It's been 40 years since I been down this road.
    Paloma, my girl friend, lived right through that gap."

We turn on the road to Terlingua and stop to look
    toward some brindled Brahma cross-cows . . .
Come in out of the desert country to Terlingua Creek
    to shade up under the cottonwoods at noontime.
"Here by this spring," Bill Bryan says,
    "I'll bet my grandaddy watered his horse a few times.

He's buried in that country toward the southeast,
    near Boquillas by the Big Bend.
His grave is by the side of this new paved road.
    They called him Jesse Parker.

He was cutting guayule on a ridge top in June.
    His horse came in. That was the first they knew
    something was wrong.
It's quite a way from here to Boquillas

and hot as it gets in June . . .
By the time the horse showed up,
    his body sure must have been a mess."

Blue bonnet blooming beside the road,
    yellow poppies just barely swaying.
A butterfly crossing in the morning sunlight . . .
    "Nobody knows what happened."

COW TRADIN' BY THE RIO GRANDE

Drum Hadley

Phil Statler had a bunch of cows sold to Ted Robb
    but some of the cows got the jimmys
    from eatin' poisoned weed and was a tremblin'
    and a shakin' and about to die.
"I'll buy every son-of-a-bitch that walks
    off the trucks alive," Ted Robb said.

Well about forty of 'em walked off the trucks and
    lay down and died. Old Ted got mad and
    didn't want to pay.

"I thought you'd take every son-of-a-bitch
    that walked off the trucks alive," Phil Statler said.
"They may have walked off," Ted Robb said.
    "But they was dead sons-a-bitches while
    they was a walkin'."

Gathering Cattle for the Fish Creek Cattle Association Before the Snows Trap Them in the High Country
Winter, Jackson Hole 1979, Wyoming

Drum Hadley

A few snow flakes falling here,
    light, clean smell of the wind in the sage.
"It takes these cold nights to make a good day,"
    Lester Jacobsen, Melody Ranch foreman, says.

Melting frost on the wheat grasses
    turning to dewdrops in the first morning sunlight.
"We had a pretty hard, cold Winter last year," Lester says,
"There's sure gonna be lots of new babies
    in Jackson Hole this Fall."

Cattle drift ahead of our horses' hooves
    drifting down the trails past Slate Creek, Crystal Creek.
Brown backs of Hereford cows, snowy clouds on the Teton Peaks,
    Crystal Flats to Horsetail
    Along the Gros Ventre River trail.

Across the river through those falling, yellow aspen leaves
    cows and calves go to slip away.

Clouds of steam and mists drift from the warm springs we pass,
　　　drift off over the scattered snows.

A Longhorn bull jumps the fence onto a highway past Kelly,
　　　starts all the bulls to fighting,
scatters cows and calves over the slick paved road
　　　where a big white semi-truck waits to pass.

"We'll pick 'em up tomorrow.
　　　Leave 'em here," Lester says,
"By that cottonwood tree just past the Mormon Road
　　　where the old buck-rail fence runs in from the West.

"When these cold snows start flyin', the cows come a trailin'
　　　past the parks and through the mountain passes.
"They come a trailin'. They've been there before.
　　　They know the way, one followin' after the other . . .

　　　　　Just as smooth as a school marm's leg."

LOOKIN' FOR A PLACE TO BED DOWN

DRUM HADLEY

Louis and Louise Taylor had been makin' all the bars
    in Douglas one Saturday night and
    Aileen saw Louise the next day.

Louise's face was all blue and puffed up
    and she could just barely see out of one eye.

Aileen asked Louise, "What happened?"

"Well," said Louise, "I come into my room
    in the Palamar Hotel last night, and
    I seen my bed just a goin' around and around the room.

I stood there and watched that bed go by a few times.
    I said, 'You sucker you, I'll catch you on the next round.'

I just ploughed right into the wall. Oh well.
    Sometimes it's hard to find a good place to bed down."

GRAND CANYON

Drum Hadley

From this rimrock edge two courting ravens
dive, twist, fall outward . . .
Outward past white rock buttes, past broken shards of mesas,
shattered mountain beyond mountain.

The drop and fall of red-cut ledge beyond ledge
sliding off . . .
toward the end of the Earth.
Blue sky, white cloud, the wind and emptiness,

Deep deep down
the rapids sounds echos . . .
rim to rimrock roaring flows of the old river,
a wind beneath two raven wings.

Hand in hand a man and woman stand together watching,
grains of sand . . . wandering toward the sea.
A trembling bridge to cross this emptiness,
piñon trees and sunlight,

you and me.

SHIPWRECK, NEW MEXICO

CYNTHIA J. HARPER

It's hard to be a cowboy's kid.
I mean, let's face it, they don't
hold rodeos in fancy places.
I asked Daddy how come this
place is called Shipwreck
if there is no ocean and no ships.
Daddy said, "Hush child,
it's only 50 miles to the Motel Six.
Just hush, there can't be an
answer for everything."

PRACTICALITY

JIM HAMMONS

"If he humps up to buck,
step down
and kick him in the belly."

Were the rancher's words
to the
green cowboy on a cold morning

Words neither cruel nor kind,
just motivated
by the will to survive

A bucking horse wastes energy
and work
isn't done by a broken Hand.

UNCLE

LINDA M. HASSELSTROM

He sips coffee
thick hands wrapped around the cup.
"This generation ain't got no corner on violence."
His sunburned hands, cracked and broken, clench into fists.
"You'd be surprised how many fellas
turned up in their own wells
in the Dirty Thirties."

The drought was less severe, he says,
here where ranchers did not tear the sod with plows.
Most families had enough to eat.
His battered hands fixed fences,
drove the teams swathing hay,
paid worn bills for the land of those who left.

Now they call him a land baron.
"Quitters," he says. "They gave up.
But someone had to stay—
and that took guts. Men like that
had hot tempers, and did
their own law-making."

DROUGHT YEAR

Linda M. Hasselstrom

I dreamed I slept alone in a drought year,
and now I do.
I lie in the short grass;
water is a dream.
All day I was fuel for the sun
burning like wildfire over a dry land.
Ghosts of streams slash earth,
water's memory
ripples in sandstone.

I dreamed you died in a drought year,
and you did. Now
I dream water all night long:
hear it laughing in the throat of a cloud,
imagine dry grass brushing the house
is rain. When the killdeer cries
at the edge of the dry pond,
I add my plea to hers
in a voice husky with dust.

I dreamed myself a dry woman,
and I am, the juice gone
out of me. My skin is fragrant
with prairie odors.
I am drying grass, wind-bent.

Long tough roots grapple
deep into baked prairie earth.
Leaves die, but roots dream
in crumbled sod,
wait for rain.

SPRING

LINDA M. HASSELSTROM

Spring is here:
the first skunk lies dead
at the highway's rim,
white fur still bright,
nose stained with one drop of blood.

A calf born dead yesterday
was found by coyotes in the night
only the head and one front foot remains.
The cat preens in a pile of meadowlark feathers.
A blue jay is eating baby robins.
The hens caught a mouse in their corn
this morning; pecked it to shrieking shreds.

It's spring;
time to kill the kittens.
Their mewing blends with the meadowlark song.
I tried drowning them once;
it was slow, painful.
Now I bash each with a wrench,
once, hard.

Each death makes a dull sound,
going deep in the ground
without
reverberations.

DIGGING POTATOES

Linda M. Hasselstrom

I

We divided it all, but
my grandmother's shoes wouldn't fit
anyone but me.
                    She'd walked years
to the old stove with firewood,
to the chickenhouse for eggs,
to the pasture to check the cows.

II

We buried her in the fall, dry
grasses blowing on the hilltop.
There were no leaves to rustle; no trees
can grow on that dry hill. The view is clear
to the river, the gumbo hills beyond.
                    We even
divided the bright spring flowers—
the hothouse roses, carnations—that
blanketed her coffin. I dropped a rosebud
as if by accident.

III

Wearing her shoes, I'm digging potatoes.
The sweet, rotten earth smell reaches up;
soil clings to my fingers, to the red
potatoes I drop in the bucket. I expect
to see her face at the bottom of each hole,
hear her voice answering the question
I've barely begun to ask.

LOVE LETTERS
LINDA HUSSA

"Wow!" was written in the dust
        on the bedside table.

The dawn and I blushed together
            as your spurs
            ching
            chinged
            around the kitchen
            and you started the fire.

I stretched full length
            on the cool smoothness
            of the sheets

            a kept woman
            a moment longer.

Within an hour's time
            we'll be ahorseback
            in a long trot
            to some distant blue mountain
            hunting cows.

I'll carry your message
            close
            knowing there will come a day
I would give a year of my life
            for that . . .
                "Wow!"

NOR A BORROWER BE

LINDA HUSSA

New pickup, shiny, clean pulls into the yard
    No hay stacked three tiers high
    No jumper cables or fix-it-all tool box
        or handyman jack
        or wads of baling wire
        or cans of staples
        or hammer with pipe handle welded on
        or fork or shovel
        or pile of rusted chains
    No 30.30 resting between dining-out coyotes
    No old dog on the seat along for the ride.

A new pickup with three men inside
    shoulder to shoulder
    stiff clothes with ironed creases
    stiff faces with importance.

Walking out to meet them
    a man in worn clothes that know sweat, not starch
    rough hand
        that sends a loop surely
        pulls a colt sweetly
        seals a deal
        changes a wheel
        and bleeds
    is extended politely
    to men
        who won't meet his eyes.

Inside the woman
>	sets out cream and sugar and cups for coffee
>	as if in welcome

Banker's eyes that look past people
>	to the bottom line
>	dissect her books with retractable scalpels
>	ask for supporting documents she can not find
>	shame her ignorant, high school concepts
>>		disappearing cash flow
>>		five year projections
>>		unrealistic budget
>	as if
>>		the six year drought
>>		rising costs
>>		doubling taxes
>>		market downturns
>>		found their origin somewhere in this house.

The brutal silence of retribution
>	of computer models projecting failure to pay
>	sell down or else
>	as years of work wadded up in pages of red ink.

And when those men are gone
>	two stone people
>	in bitter silence
>	the hurt so deep
>	there is no solace
>	in each other's arms

SEWING CIRCLE

Linda Hussa

Use the long curving needle
　　　better for speed and it's sharp
Start with a slip stitch
　　　no need to sew blind, simply sew it
　　　and gentle, be gentle.

Pull soft where the pieces are missing
　　　time will fill in the rest
Begin and just sew
　　　it's slippery, I know. Quickly
　　　work quickly, work fast.

"Old Ned? (Lapper, Spot, Sox, Little Bess)
　　　Why, he was curled by the fire
　　　my slippers under his chin
　　　his running dreams made the children laugh
　　　never hurt a fly, that one."

My evening by the fire
>> quilting bloody flaps, pushing
>> puckers out into a whole sheep.

Five little town dogs, crazed by sport
>> follow a full moon through meadows
>> pack of shadows slide along
>> where the flock is bedded
>> until they woke to a low wail,
>> and yip.
>> We woke to their pain.

Twenty-seven little sheep, dazed by death
>> strewn, whimpering
>> —sheep whimper when hurt, like us—
>> three floating in the pond, one gutted
>> fine white wool dyed a vomitus shade
>> of red.

By a flashlight's fire
>> we sewed them, skinned faces
>> jaws flapping, legs waving
>> our anger seared by the task.

So, you say it wasn't old Ned, (Blackie,
>> Irish, Tommy or Princess)
>> I stood under the porch light
>> and I handed over Ned's collar
>> strands of bloody wool in the catch.

WAITING
LINDA HUSSA

Beside the table sitting
the ivy has a new leaf since yesterday
when she sat there
in the heartbreaking silence.

The jay is standing in the seed box
kicking like an old hen hunting worms.
She should take her Daisy BB gun
     and pop him in the britches
but doesn't move
because she's waiting.

Fifty odd years of marriage
taught her to wait
for his return,
for the rattley noise his truck made
     from the $\frac{1}{2}$ mile away
     down the canyon.
Even the old black dog recognized it.
He would get up out of the dust,
     stretch,
     walk out,
     yawn,
     and sit down to wait.

She waited for the last word on his daily itinerary
        and made her plans then.
It was a partnership
        with him the major stockholder.

She silently steered his life
        a deep strong current
        the ship had no power against
        taking him across latitudes not on his charts.
She waited with him for the doctor
        then she helped him wait to die.

Now she must undo that thing inside her
        that tells her to wait.

THE MAN SHOEING A HORSE AND HIS LITTLE GIRL

Linda Hussa

He whirled those blue eyes on me
       flat blue eyes
       bottomless eyes
       where the pupil had shrunk up so he was only seeing through
that pinhole
       screwing me down like a microscope seeing into me past
awkward structural uprights, joist and 2x4, past electrical wires
running, past grey puttied pipes, past insulation, wall board,
paint, plaster, and chimney into the real center—the blueprint
where angles could be altered to add or subtract things, and I
felt myself shrinking, all jellied with no legs to run

       but those eyes
       in that face flushed red by his frustration and the hoof
ripped through his knees

       seemed to wash calm
       the pupil coiled out and was the dark seeing center
       with the thin blue wall
       no more X-ray vision

       and those blue eyes
       ran over me like warm honey
       smeared me
       the rasping palm
       soft

smoothed me out so I wasn't sorry anymore I asked the
question and he

in that voice

I could pull on and wear

spoke

AMERICAN HERO—*For Cary*

BILL JONES

A reluctant war story
It came in yearly pieces

Four blindfolded Vietcong prisoners
Bleat
On a Huey floor
Before the boot
Of a strutting Vietnamese Colonel
Kicks the first one into whistling

      E m p t i n e s s.

The second
      Then the third
But the fourth
Babbles above the rotor whine
Invents desperate
Elaborate
Fantasy answers.

But it makes no difference
As the Colonel winks
And gives the final shove.

"You are too dumb to be afraid."
Admiral Zumwalt grins
Pins on his
            fourth
Silver Star
Moves down the column
Leaving the half-truth
Floating
            in a timeless wake.

On a Wyoming butte
            two decades away
We stop to rest horses—
Antelope weave the hills.
"What about the medals?" I ask.

"Oh, those
I threw them away
A long   long
Time Ago."

LUCK OF THE DRAW—*For Warren Spriggs*

BILL JONES

There were a thousand
White eyed leaping broncos
Smoke stale single rooms
Small town arenas
Full of dust and promise
Then the Accident
Split five decades
To Before and the
Unthinkable
After.

He rolls expertly now
Tires squeaking faintly
Between glass cases of
Arapahoe beadwork
Rows of rusted traps
Peddling second hand guns
Postcards, souvenirs
And stories of the old days.

The deck went cold
And all agree
That the gut twisting fall
From a first place win
In Cheyenne Frontier Days

Great Wild Horse Race
To a rubber wheeled chair
Is a distance
Impossible to measure

But as woodfires glow crimson
And frozen winter nights
Cast dull mountain shadows
Sleep gives life to dreams
Withered limbs and long dead hope
He rides the wild ponies
Hoofs pounding hollow rhythms
Flat-out
In the lead
Invincible

LOOKING BACK

TERESA JORDAN

The secret place is gone.
Picked up like a tenant
in the middle of the night
after a bad run of luck
it trudges down the dark lone road
with the meadow
and the barn
and a long line of cows,
tails bedraggling behind them.
I loved

that secret place
down by the riverbed
hidden by a bank. I whittled
dolls from willows there, made whistles
out of broad bladed grass, told my big bay
Buddy how I'd never leave.
I lied

though not from will.
Let me be salt
sculpted by cow
tongues until I am lace
and then I am gone.

I want to belong to the ground
again. It is the barn

that breaks my heart
trudging soddenly along, bedsteads
and broken harnesses rocking
softly in the loft, lost
beneath great drifts of
guano. A spavined horse-
collar mirror hangs
cockeyed on the ladder
and that other me looks back
amazed. In the darkness
only one of us is
gone.

OLD ANNE

Teresa Jordan

The arm that hadn't healed right would not bend
to hold a hairbrush. "Hack it off!"
Old Anne said of her braid, that braid like blood
flung from the heart, so long a part of her
that thick grey snake slung heavy down her back.
Young Charlotte, wide-eyed Charlotte, stroked the shears,
reached out her hand to touch the braid, drew back—
"Please, child," Anne said, "don't be afraid to help me."
So Charlotte cut, and Old Anne closed her grey
sun-tired eyes. The hacking made her think
of falling, the colt falling, rain-soaked limestone soil
slick as oil—slicker—and a boulder field
cut jagged at the bottom of the hill.
The heavy braid hung loosely now by just a few thin strands;
The scissors sawed one last time through, it fell.
The soft thud she remembered just before
she woke, before the pain set in; the young horse,
stunned, on top of her, had just begun to twitch.

DO NOT ASK

Greg Keeler

Do not ask for whom they moo
or why they stand and chew and chew.
They've got their plans; their heads are clear.
Their future moves from mouth to rear.
Somewhat like ours (like ours I mean
who see no more than what we've seen,
who do our best till noon then run
to eat that beef between those buns
then do our best into the night
before the T.V.'s tiny light).
They munch the purple clover in
then splatter it right out again,
not quite as pretty as it was,
at most a place for flies to buzz.
But God, they're stable on four feet,
no philosophical elite
to make them wonder why they chew
and urinate the way they do
or sit and ponder what they're worth.
No, cows just occupy the earth:
the same earth, by the way, which one
fine day will melt into the sun.

LLAMAS IN THE LANDSCAPE

GREG KEELER

And what are these
spattering calico
over this valley
of the Horse Shoe Hills
at the True West confluence
of the Missouri headwaters?
These big cuties—
some kind of cross
between an ostrich
and a pet-shop bunny—
have come of age
tiptoeing among
the mares and geldings.
So take that saddle
off ol' Buck,
and throw a pack or two
on Sweetie and Foofoo.
The range has never
been so homey as
under these dainty puffballs,
ears straight up
and noses sniffing
thin air.
And sorry ol' Paint,
but your hooves,
your flat iron clodhoppers
are too fat and careless
for what's left
of the trail.
Yes bring on Phoebe

and Fauntleroy
floating over their bird-toes
like mottled baloons,
leaving the path intact
for this new age
of huge moist eyes
and batting eyelashes—
a spit for a nicker,
John Wayne in drag.

COYOTE'S WILDERNESS LOBBY

Greg Keeler

Dog, Pony and Coyote
went to Capital Hill
to lobby. Together,
Dog and Pony lobbied
for dog and pony shows.
In private, Dog lobbied
for lenient policies
for pooping in public places,
and Pony lobbied for leg traps
to catch coyotes. Coyote
lobbied for more wilderness.
Dog wound up with a top job
in the BLM, and Pony headed up
the Department of the Interior.
Coyote brought up the rear,
glumly clanking a leg trap
behind him down
the capital steps.

WHAT'S LEFT OF THE WEST

GREG KEELER

Manifest Destiny ain't had a rest
Since Horace Greeley said, "Young Man, go west."
So we've chewed up the mountains and spit out the plains
While we get indigestion with each acid rain.
It's gotten so bad, the West ain't any place;
I'll ask you how are you, and you stare into space.
What's left of the West where we've already been?
So I'll ask ya, how are ya, again.

> *Honolulu's no lulu, Fairbank's ain't so fair;*
> *Take a sip of the water, take a whiff of the air,*
> *Take some pictures of the wildlife, take a leak in a stream,*
> *Take a jet back to Cleveland and dream.*

If trees ran for Congress and forests could vote,
Our chances of survival might not be so remote;
Since we don't give a damn about how they'd elect
Their absentee ballots have a greenhouse effect.
What's a boatload of timber, what's the whole human race?
I'll ask you how are you, and you stare into space.
What's left of the West where we've already been?
So I'll ask ya, how are ya, again.

Honolulu's no lulu, Fairbank's ain't so fair;
Take a sip of the water, take a whiff of the air,
Take some pictures of the wildlife, take a leak in a stream,
Take a jet back to Cleveland and dream.

We scrub up with phosphates and flush down the suds
Till the banks of our rivers are bubbles and mud;
Just to stay sanitary we've gone to these lengths—
Now our whole ecosystem is industrial strength.
It's so simple to screw up what can't be replaced.
I'll ask you how are you, and you stare into space.

What's left of the West where we've already been?
So I'll ask ya, how are ya, again.

Honolulu's no lulu, Fairbank's ain't so fair;
Take a sip of the water, take a whiff of the air,
Take some pictures of the wildlife, take a leak in a stream,
Take a jet back to Cleveland and dream.

TEMPTATION

MIKE LOGAN

You think you know temptation
'Cause you've seen the city lights
Or the gleam of easy money
Or some dance hall girls in tights?

You think you know temptation?
Well, boys, I'm tellin' you,
'Til you've rode a horse to school in spring,
You haven't got a clue.

'Til you've seen the breaks a greenin'
An' the days is warmin' up
An' you're ten years old, ahorseback,
Followed by your fav'rite pup.

'Til the meadowlarks is singin'
An' a leadin' you both on
An' the dandylion's is bloomin'
By a newborn whitetail fawn.

'Til you know there's lessons waitin'
In the schoolhouse just for you,
But the crick's a siren callin'
An' the sky's its deepest blue.

'Til you see a pair of greenwings
Or a baby cottontail
Or a killdeer fakes a broken wing
To lead you off the trail.

'Til your horse kicks up an arrowhead,
Down near the bison kill,
Or he tries the road that swings around
The old bootlegger's still.

'Til your pup's a chasin' butterflies
Or huns up in the draw
Or a work horse colt comes wobblin' up,
On new legs, with his ma.

'Til the sage hens is a struttin'
On the hill beside the school
An' the thought of learnin' hist'ry
Seems a fate unjust an' cruel.

Now them is real temptations,
Not like the lust for gold
Or the mad desire for power
That can seize you when you're old.

You think you know temptation?
Well, boys, I'm tellin' you,
'Til you've rode a horse to school in spring,
You haven't got a clue.

ROCK-SOLID WOMEN—*For Luisina*

JO-ANN MAPSON

Gemma's dead, but her presence scrubs the kitchen
        to a sheen blinding as resurrection. I'm to sleep in

her bed, dream dreams wild as the pure silver
        shocking her black hair at sixteen. Like greedy mares,

we're all after sugar. "Kisses from the wrong men
        generally taste best——" when it came to kissing,

Gemma had her sugar. Her scent, all woman, seasoned in grief,
        won't fade. Like I'm supposed to

take home all I've given her. How
        do I pack the dark-skinned madonna,

handkerchiefs, old wedding photos, images that won't
        fold like her body, drained of blood,

eager for earth to cool in? I can't find
        a suitcase for Gemma's instruction:

clumsily crease my how to's: conjure dignity from the glint
        of policeman's badge, tough out a path

through mile-long years of shit, just plain shit.
        But the copper blazes here in the kitchen.

Ain't grief productive? Women cleaning. Dresser scarves
        stiffen. Her amethyst rosary sways from an old nail,

good crystal sparkling behind wavering glass.
        Upstairs, brown wallpaper tongues peel

from hundred-year-old walls that know
        all my secrets. Soon someone else will

live here, discard gifts, room with the silence
        I learned. When her heart stopped

I understood how everything happens behind curtains:
        making daughters, turning to rock-solid women,

because even during sex we prop up men. We were never
        racehorses, more the draft breed, dully pulling

on the yoke, surely just another bone to the shoulder.
        Please say the grudge isn't all we hold between us.

TIME BEFORE WINTER

JO-ANN MAPSON

Longing grows anywhere,
its nearest relative the thistle.
Whole summers, I could sit
for hours studying nothing,
noting like a feeble botanist
the approximate
hour sunflowers closed up shop,
yellow petals hoarding
the fat brown pistil.
Grasshoppers ate
through whatever I planted, the hay turned
amber where sun hit each bale
because the barn roof needed mending,
but always there was time,
time before winter.

Our horses took the hills
when asked, learned that a pressing leg
meant we would turn together
through mountain lupine, blue
as lake water. There were flowers
I would not name for fear of autumn
taking you from me, back to the cattle,
to winter range land free of women.
On the fire road, the bright flash

of a Coke can fading in sunlight
crunched underhoof, startling the mare,
sending me flying.
You said "Bones will heal,"
as I lay in silt
practicing how to believe you
for the long ride home.

Now this same light, imported,
another August, bronzing my skin
and breaking the shadows,
splices memory into my blood
when far off heat lightning
incises the horizon,
paints the barn roof the color
of your leaving. With my healed bones
propped by the light of kerosene
lantern, I want to believe you're coming
back. My foolish heart loads
each chamber with facile poetry,
drinks hope down like a thermos
of cowboy coffee, stutters through
night alone, scouting.

POOR MAN'S SILVER—*for Sultan*

JO-ANN MAPSON

This is not the way it's supposed to end,
you down in the pasture, fighting twisted gut,

the office transposing the 6 and the 8
in my phone number, the vet forcing enemas,

electrolyte IV's like prayer, two full hours
before dawn, a friend's call waking me,

25 miles of rush hour traffic, the laughing guy
in the Toyota, his radio blaring Howard Stern.

We were supposed to have one last gallop
down a smuggler's trail, reckless as thieves,

no fences, together, instead I arrive in time
to see your tail, the only part not covered by tarp,

and sit by your cooling carcass
so I can write a check for a man who will skin

your hide to be boiled into glue, grind
your hooves into Bisquick and Jell-O,

some earthly agony they call ascension.

NOTES ON AGING

JO-ANN MAPSON

Beneath me he slows, halts,
cocks a hind leg and dozes.
Have I always been on his back? I wonder
what he dreams, spotted skin twitching,
metal shoes sinking into old sand.

I scan my hands for age spots,
find three and panic. I can't blame
the sun, I'm sure not Appaloosa.
Bridle leather eventually rots;
no matter how much oil I rub,
every stitch frays.

He kicks at the fence. I weep for no good
reason. Moons replace each other,
snakes sleep out the season.
Oaks leaf out, green under the bulldozer.
Rolled oats glisten in the bucket
telling you again
to relish the run,
keep charging those fences.
Molasses is a first kiss.
Dream about it for fifty years,
you grow wise.

for souls

ROD MCQUEARY

Perhaps,
He said, it's not a man's heart or mind
That drives him down to surging sea
To straining mast.
Not mind, he said, that makes him fill
Some quivering stirrup   eagerly
To float across the grunting
Pounding range,
Hat fanning reckless, loose and fast.
Not mind that sends him high
            beyond the tether of the wind   or cloud,

Spear through the air   to ride the sky,
            ascend the stairs, forsake the sod
To loose the reins and challenge   proud
Or taste the salty tears of God.
Perhaps it's not the heart   or mind
That spurs us on from thrill to thrill

But fluttering soul   stretching, straining,
Caged by ribs and blood   but still
Impatiently   but uncomplaining
Hopes for some escape to find.
Beneath some struggling bronco's death
In a tortured metal fuselage

Or sinking calm 'neath raging wave
Past the pain   and fear   and breath
We learn how new-freed souls behave.
Released now by this mortal's death
Unconfined by time or space,
Brighter, lighter, upward cast,
Newborn, it wakes in a chromed tunnel
Just beyond Medusa's face
And wonders why—It's free   at last.
Great God almighty,   Free
. . . at last.

WORK FOR FOOD

ROD MCQUEARY

Where highways
93 and 40 cross
         a 4-way stop
         an overpass
I interrupt my hurry, north
To notice this solitary
         Man.
He's paunchy, pigtail grey
                 and that
         Sickly, indoor kind
         of pale,
His bulbous, pockmarked
Nose
         Tells much.
He holds a cardboard sign
         (magic marked) that
Begs—Viet Vet—Work for Food.
He (and it) hold my eye, and
         I wonder hard
         About this man.
The miles   the years
         Have blurred the green
         Bent the Memories
         (and Minds)
         to suit
He can probably recite
The Names, the outfits
That climbed some hard-won

Hill—and gave it back.
Knows somebody who knows
Somebody who knows   you

It's getting hard
To tell an honest, grizzled
      Ex-Hero
      Who sucks cheap wine
      and yearns for youth
      and the
      Innocence
We once were
      all too glad
To lose,
      from a
Common, grungy, middle-aged
      Drunk
Who knows which words
      Will work
I take the smooth, Corporate
      Cowardly
Escape.
I have a truck to chase,
Cows to sort for tomorrow's
      Beef auction
      In Jerome.
I have responsibilities.
So   I roll through
      The stop   and
      Save . . . the wave.

POINT OF NO RETURN

ROD McQUEARY

Loading possessions
Sorting for the journey
Go and stay

My hands are steady
Heart is calm
The many miles between us
Cannot detract from who we are
    or might have been.

Would I change us
Cut rough edges to fit?
Like the perfect linoleum seam,
Flush enough to appear
Invisible?

No.

Life is the reward for
Where we've been, what we did,
How much we grew.

It's past the point of
No return.
Beyond Recalling
Energy gone kinetic
Outside the bounds of human shaping.
A wild God
takes a deep breath.

Bronc Riders, Gunfighters know well
That elongated instant
Where reality stretches like a placenta.
Time curves through a prism of
Adrenaline and joy,
Fear falls earthward
Like the innocence.

He deliberately slides the sixth
Shell into the empty chamber.
Turns away from an empty glass,
Loop off the hammer
Feels the reassuring weight on hip
Tugs hat brim for
Perhaps
The last time.
Blinks to keen the eyes
Pushes swing doors outward
To clear the view of silent street.

Handful of horn, it's easy up
Right boot cuts a perfect arc
Over steel hard trembling
Hip muscles,
Toe reaching to embrace off stirrup.
Spurred foot falls faster
Now
Hips swivel to meet the leather
"Watch his ears, always watch his ears"

Just one more instant.
The wait is almost
Over.

NO APOLOGIES

ROD MCQUEARY

Somewhere along the way
You have noticed warnings
Caught a dead scent whiff
Of old miseries,
Old agonies
Not so long, not so gone.
It is your right,
Your obligation
To protect your piece
Of hard won freedom.

You give unmistakable
Body language signals
And this deaf man
Obliges with pocketed hands,
No more jokes, and
Two steps backward,
Now.

It was great, when it was great,
And after that,
It was mostly OK, like
Sundown, loose rein,
Riding tired horses home.

I know the sleepless
Analyzing nights
Serve no purpose.
Still, some linear logic,
Reptilian, guitar string,
Trip-wire sensitivity
Wonders where
I accidently stepped,
That sent things

Wrong.

THE PANHANDLE

LARRY MCWHORTER

Where the short grass struggles daily,
Racing wind to claim each rain
Before it sucks the precious drops
Up in it's skyward drain.

Where the humblest of dreamers,
Bent on shaping sod to plow,
Saw dusters claim their visions.
They're all just mem'ries now.

Out here the deer and antelope
Are working all the time.
They seldom get the chance to play
As in the age old rhyme.

This land is harsh and brutal.
Winters cold, the summers hot.
It metes out oh so little,
While demanding all you've got.

The tourists heading east or west,
In haste to get across,
Don't stop except for food or gas,
So, it's not a total loss.

THE LONELY MEN

NEIL MEILI

Their little dark houses still dotted the
prairie
when I was growing up.

They all seemed to cling to the soil as if
their life force had all been used up in the
long
and difficult transplanting, and they
could hang on but no longer grow.

Or they stood alone surrounded by sadness
and the small and smaller markers of what
had fallen to the reapers scythe.

Their roots loosened year after year by
the hot winds and the deep frosts they
became more and more brittle until one by
one
they broke off like tumbleweeds
and were gone.

MEMORIES OF THREE OR FOUR
NEIL MEILI

I remember being nestled in that old ranch
kitchen, deep in the warmth of washday
monday.
The maytag's liquid sound mixing with the
gentle driving chugs of the little gas engine,
sloshing and chugging, sloshing and chugging as
I curled up beside it in the great pile of
laundry rich with the smells of the people I
loved.
Half asleep, half awake, I floated there, all my
senses safely cradled and warmed and part of
a rhythm and a sound like a heartbeat in a
womb.

THRESHING TIME
NEIL MEILI

I remember at Christmas getting a great toy threshing machine.
A block of wood with wooden spools nailed to the side
but I loved it as I loved the threshing

All through the long summer days I would walk the fields with my dog.
At night my mother rubbed strong liniment on four-year-old legs.
Growing pains she said, although one always hurt more
and didn't seem to grow any faster.

And the grain grew too, and passed me, and was higher than I was
and then harvest, and the wonder of it falling to the binder
and the magic of the machine as it tied the sheaves
and ke-chunked them into the carrier.

And the stooking——little teepees covering the prairie again
and the golden warmth of everything.

And the threshing machine; they wouldn't let me too close, it might eat
    me
like it ate those sheaves and like the men in the crew could eat
and they could eat even when it rained,

While I sat for hours, nose to wet window
watching the long nosed monster
deep in the timeless mists

And hot clear windless days when everything sang and the big belt
    slapped
and the machine came to life again and wagons were on both sides
and the big horses were standing strong and ready
and switching flies; with dignity.

The sun caught the arch of the long plume of straw and the chaff lifting
and the old hands fed the machine in a sort of easy sweat oiled rhyme
and the new hands stood on the sheaves they tried to lift each time

And the old hands laughed, and the new hands laughed
and they were men together.

THE CROW

NEIL MEILI

TWO BOYS   AND CROW   AT 50 YARDS

TWO SHOTS   AS ONE THE CROW   FELL STILL

WE LAUGHED   AND RAN   WHOSE HIT? WHOSE MISS?

TWO HOLES IN HEAD

AS CLOSE AS

THIS

OO

THE LIFE WAS IN OUR EYES AND SKILL

TOO FAR FROM DEATH TO UNDERSTAND A KILL

THE LESSON

Wayne Nelson

He was grouchier than usual that day,
Expected me to read his mind,
Didn't give me time to adjust the stirrups,
To my longer than his,
Teenage lanklegs,
Just shoved the lariat in my hands,

Usually,
Content to stay on the ground, I
Liked to wrestle calves,
Felt clumsy with a rope in my hands, But
There was one calf left to brand, and
He suddenly decided,
I was BY GOD going to rope it,

Took forever to get the twists
Out of the loop,
He jerks it back, shoves a perfect loop,
Back at me in a millisecond,

"How did you——?"
"Go rope that goddamn calf! We got fence to fix!
If you didn't spend all your time hangin' around
those pissy-assed town kids you'd learn somethin'!"

So that was it
That's why your pale blue eyes burned at me all day,

Threading through the milling, bawling herd,
Finally see the little soon to be steer,
Without the fresh black CN QUARTERCIRCLE crust,

Touch heels to Snip, break into a lope
Cutting him away from his mother, swing the loop
Twice, stand up in
The Old Man's
Too short stirrups and cast.
The loop hovers momentarily, like a vulture
Over his whitefaced head and drops.
Jerk my slack, the calf's body whips backward
Starting a dally while I tug on the reins,
Snip comes to a bouncing stop. My trunk lurches
Forward, positioning my family life directly
Above that weathered old Thomas horn.
Once, twice, three times
It becomes an anvil
Designed to flatten my testicles.

Blinding pain, nausea,

The damn rope slips, forgotten, out of the dally
And away, leaving me hunched over with my face
Buried in Snip's somehow understanding black mane.
Behind me I hear
The Old Man's
Sour chuckle as he says to my Big Brother:
"He ropes like Ma fishes."

THE MURDER OF CROWS

JENNIFER OLDS

Shots rang out and birds
spun down like rain,
a heavy black hail of crows.
Blood bright bodies flopped
in gravel as he wept,
aimed, fired, reloaded
and did it all again.

After fifteen years he'd had
enough grief in the spring;
bandit crows pillaging the fruitless
mulberry for nests of hatchling sparrows.
Fifteen years of featherless birds
tumbling to splash open on
the ground as crows kited down to gorge.
That time, something shining
snapped open in his mind
and he shot them out like lights.

At nightfall he gathered the bodies
and buried them beneath
the flowers by the bridle path.
Each year his roses swam
higher and neighbors paused
on horseback to lean down
and pay homage.
His face queered, paled.

He said it was the crows.

CULLING THE HERD

JENNIFER OLDS

When the new chick flopped
wretched from its shell
(hatched without skin
or the possibility of feathers),
its hen kicked it
to the center of the yard,
plucked at its eyes
and the pecking began.
In the barn, a slant-eyed cat
queened an odd one out,
winkled it from the others
and ate it.

This is how a herd is culled;
the pure and impure separated
to live or die,
each according to its form.

Still, there are exceptions.
The bay mare who dropped
a blind foal and,
not knowing the flaw,
understood that there was one
and bared her teeth
to chase off the herd

then used those molars
to grip its neck
and guide it to her side.

In the big house
a boy child was born
without speech or sound and,
in a hellish lurch,
she recalled the culling
then shoved it off,
rubbed his poor dead ears
and bundled him close
and nursed him.

IN THE TIME OF THE PLAGUE

JENNIFER OLDS

Risk as adventure:
Jumping the gray mare
over tumbleweeds,
no saddle or bridle,
you burred to her back
in a sweat-legged grip.
Later, ten cowboys
in the back of a truck,
ropes hissing the air
as we let fly, dallied,
turned every street sign in town.
When the cops flashed us
near the park, we scattered;
lucky us diving into the dugout
as the searchlights swung past.

Risk as real danger:
Pumping 100
through the Hollywood Hills
drunk on tequila and wind,
missing a curve
for a moment's long dangle
over a cliff's crumbling edge.
That, I thought, surely
closed book on the word.
But in '85 you tugged down
your pants for a stranger.
Now you lay tented.
I hold your hand.
Read Keats. Slowly.

REASONS FOR RAIN

BARBARA SHIRK PARISH

We gather today on the doorstone
as the thunderstorm begins.
Grandad is speaking: "This rain
is Holy Water
blessing our fields and sowing
its river seeds. It is an answered prayer:
Last night I dreamed in German
that the terrible drouth would end."

Grandma is bowing her head
but Aunt Annie mutters, "This is the rain I predicted
when the pony rolled over and the cattle
kicked up their heels."

NIGHT LEGACY

BARBARA SHIRK PARISH

In the one-roomed house of the Germans
the women cannot retire:
they share with the men
the talk of the ocean journey—
the unfinished work on the prairie;
and the children asleep in the dark
hear not of the terrible winters,
the myths of the midwives,
the typhoid, the rivers gone dry—
but when they wake up and grow old
they will remember.

GRANDMOTHER'S LAND

BARBARA SHIRK PARISH

Hers is a land unsettled—
touched only by the sundown
and the dawn;

a trumpet vine unites
her house with earth

while fallow fields
lie dreaming
of the seed.
Her high plains
lift our spirits—stretch
our imaginations;

mountains rise
in the distance
to welcome her children home.

MY GRANDFATHER'S AND FATHER'S HORSES

SHADD PIEHL

*Whether drifting through life on a boat or climbing toward old age
leading a horse, each day is a journey and the journey itself is home.*
—Basho

> The two old-timers stand out west of town
> With maybe a few cows to share
> A bale and ground feed each morning.
> King, over thirty, is swaybacked, slow
> And still impossible to catch
> (except by tricks, women and oats).
> Cheese, once a terror in the corral,
> Now no longer rules the roost.
> In their old age they shy,
> Meeting themselves in shadows
> At the water trough.
> Both needing their teeth floated,
> Dun horses out to pasture,
> Every cowboy has a horse that's not for sale.

STORM FRONT

SHADD PIEHL

1.
The colt noses the water,
Paws, muddies the creek.
At my insistence he gathers
And crosses in a great lunge.
I grab leather as we crash
Over tangles of buffalo brush,
Leaving the draw in crow-hop leaps.
I am glad we are alone and unseen.

2.
On top, grey clouds the sun,
Trails smokey veils of rain.
The wind picks up mane, jumps
Through grass, sings dust.
As I pull down my hat, the dun
Raises his head and cries to horses
On dark hills. Along the storm front
A red-tailed hawk hangs still.

3.
I chuck us into a slow lope,
Then into a cold falling wall.
Letting the colt have his head,
I hide mine beneath hat brim, in
A fool's trust of a three-year-old.

The world becomes one of sound
And touch, between myself and earth
The running horse. Thunder

4.
Explodes beneath the mist;
I watch grass blur past.
Listen—The day single-foots
As we run. Somewhere the hawk
Waits it out in a tree. The horses
Have their asses to the wind.
This rain that wets us is the same
That runs to the creek, and chills
The hawk, horses and hills.

5.
After rolling in the corral,
Does the muddied colt forget
Our run?—far horses, red hawk
And dark storm? I, again the fool,
Wonder. Was our ride the rain?
Is the creek our lives?
The braided hair rope, my macate,
Is rough and stiffens in my hands.

RIDING SONG

SHADD PIEHL

Out of the earth
I sing for them.
A horse nation
I sing for them.
Out of the earth
I sing for them.
The animals
I sing for them.
—Teton Sioux

I sit my horse
In circles
On a hill of
Half-buried stone hoops,
The forgotten remains
Of nomad lodges.
Impatient he stamps a
Red flowered cactus.
From the earth
An eagle bone whistle
Sings through the grass.
Something whispers
And I tuck it behind my ear.
Bones bleached and scattered

Tell stories of
A horse nation.
It is a good day to live
And not to grow old.
Today my pony leaves tracks
Through the past,
My heart sings a song
For yesterday
And only the hills are forever.

PAHA SAPA

SHADD PIEHL

Four old kings stare
Down their reign,
Granite men in black
Hills of emerald—
Parking lot owners
In a broken
Treaty land of
Billboards
Marine worlds and
Reptile gardens.

TOWARDS HORSES
—for Tom Mau and Kenny Taton

SHADD PIEHL

*"Bronc stompers, hell roarers
And all-around hands, going to the peelin'."*

Near Castle Butte, the clouds
Hang in wavy mare's-tails,
Appaloosa thin and carded
Against a sky with too little blue.
The plain's irrigated hay land
Has been made into round bales
That roll with us to Rapid City.
Tom is reading the Sports News.
Kenny wakes and shuffles cards
For another round of pitch.
I set the cruise at seventy-five,
And we play, past the Belle Fource,
Past Bear Butte, weaving between
Black Hills tourist winnebagos.
The air cools and becomes as charged
As they who travel towards horses,
Living the days by tokens:
Horses.   Creek.
                    Sky.
          Bronc saddles. Butte.
Never ending road.

PAINT

Thelma Poirier

Until she saw the horse, stuffed and saddled
tied to a hitching post inside a bar

she was not a believer, though someone
told her, or she had read that years ago

Roy stuffed Trigger; but this old paint,
moon blind and moth eaten

makes no pretensions; he was nobody's
rope horse, nobody's racing pride

just an old school pony, tied in a bar
for no apparent reason, yet

he leads her into dreams. Morning
finds him still tied to her bedpost.

badlands

Thelma Poirier

we want to take visitors to see grass
rough hairgrass or blue grama
it is not grass they want to see
it is badlands
dry gulches and adobe hills
streaks of color grey and rose
layers of concealed fossils
and on the surface, clumps
of primrose and sage
scattered cacti

they have heard stories of badlands
great adventures
        rustlers, outlaws
are not content with subtleties of grass
prefer badlands
        dry crotch in a sea of grass

wild flowers

THELMA POIRIER

moving to the prairies, there are things you should know
neighbours will forget to tell you

and you can not read them in the Farmer's Almanac
they are not printed on paper

the lure of wild flowers
small signals written in petal and stamen

where the larkspur grows,
how to recognize the plant before it blossoms

the purple poison; how a cow died
and three heifers aborted their calves

because no one was watching larkspur, and
another year it was a filly

chomping on a locoweed; and what of nightshade
it dealt a double death, a team of horses

wild flowers, warnings

one for the sheep

THELMA POIRIER

I met a woman in Elko
should have known she raised sheep
had more than a hundred ewes to lamb next month

there were enough signs—
her joints, knick-a-knack
as she walked across the platform

her sad eyes
the colour of California sage
her woolly hair

the way she ate the lamb at Biloxi's
almost reluctantly—tiny bites

and the way she bleated out her poems
soft as evening air
I should have known she raised sheep

a thousand miles apart
we write letters

she tells me about the ewes
bagged out and lambing
lambs, one after another stillborn
without reason

darkness filled with poetry,
her sheep camp
silent

STARLIGHT ON THE TRAIL

CHARLES POTTS

Packing in the primitive
Idaho Chamberlain Basin area south
Of the main Salmon River twenty years ago
I found myself in Moose Meadows at dark
Twelve miles from the cabin
On a trail I'd been on exactly once,

Stumbling through the moonless dark
With eight pack horses, two mules
Four extra saddle horses and one
Plumb green kid from Michigan.

I shut my eyes and sighed once
Amazed to open my eyes and see
The trail a trifle more clearly.

I rode three steps with my eyes closed
And three with them open,
Picked up enough
Starlight on the trail
To find our dark way home.

THE HOMESTEAD ACT

CHARLES POTTS

For years my sleep was tormented with dreams
Of returning to the sided log cabin I grew up in
And finding it empty, which was no dream
But the actual condition of returning each day
From high school to be alone with the dwindling livestock
And the universal daydream of running away or leaving home.

I returned to the barnyard many years later
With my four-year-old daughter Emily in my arms
to stare at the space where the barn had been
Sawed up and shipped for its weather beaten pine
To yuppie ranchettes in the greater LA Basin
And all I could feel was love.

I'd expected to be able to make sense of my life
If not then, then now, if not now then when
Strolling down September lanes with tears in my eyes
Past the place where my family's cabin burned
To the ground and I heard my brother Stan describe
In the eulogy how Dad threw milk on the
Sod-roofed logs aflame and they lived the rest of that
Depression summer in a tent with a bed and a stove.
The Burnette ditch where I frequently went
As if I didn't have solitude to burn
Was a hundred yards away and of no use to anybody
Trying to put out a fire.

No one could have guessed all the "hell and high water"
I would go through in the ensuing thirty years
Except perhaps Ogden Nash and his beautiful warm note
"Everybody knows the trouble I've seen."

I remember Idaho from some preposterous angles
With the good sense to leave out the private parts,
Unlike the other log cabin that grandpa Herb built near
Darlington with 1896 excised in the header
Still standing as a loafing shed with no foundation,
Or the Teppnyaki banquet after Dad's memorial service
Where everyone went fishing for flipped shrimp in the air.

But mostly I stick with "down the lane" to the North
Where I last walked that day with Emily
And my memories of how thin soiled, cold weathered,
High altitude, high latitude, high interest ranching
Came crashing down a no love for Lincoln Lane.

COWBOYS BETWEEN RANCHES

CHARLES POTTS

Mom and Dad auctioned their ranch in 1960
To pay the bills and go back
To teaching school and washing dishes.

Me and 50 million other
Back to the landers who lost their footing
Since the Great Depression
Would like to have the land back.

Me and my brothers provide the service,
A packer and guide, an agricultural contractor
A real, estate broker.

Hardly any cowboys own the land they ride.
Will any of us be able to afford it again?

I'll go back to my heavily mortgaged half acre
And its 3,000 head of box elder bugs,
The neighbor's five cats and the perennial raccoons.

They come down the creeks looking for
Catfood and crayfish.
Their eyes remind me of the wilderness
Glowing defiantly in the dark.

MAKE WAY FOR DANIEL BOONE

CHARLES POTTS

Is there anyone left unaware
That the planet has been poisoned,
Polluted, and permanently desecrated
By the rapacious hands of man?

My *Greenpeace* magazine flatly states
That half the heavy rock bands
Sold five million albums in the Soviet Union,
While I carry this message with the
High tech equivalent of a push broom
Through the potholed streets of Walla Walla.

Give me a break, Daniel Boone. I need
Elbow room from the rock and roll ecologists.
Imagine feeling crowded when the nearest other person
Is twelve miles away!

Put me on the front porch
Of his final frontier cabin,
Jackson County Missouri, 1803,
Some place to sulk as Lewis and Clark
Bypass my heart on their way west.

A MONKEY IN THE HIGH 90'S

CHARLES POTTS

Faced with a barrage of excited chattering,
I want so hard to believe there is
A breakthrough just around the corner,
Even though I realize *The Hundredth Monkey*
In the nuclear charade was Comrade Korbachev.

Among more than 100 suggested ways we could help
To save the planet in the recent *Utne Reader,*
Across the facing page of Christian Ecology are,
"Organize potluck dinners" and
"Be creative with leftovers."

Why not leftover potluck.
Or better still
A potluck fast:
Just bring your hunger and contemplate.

UNCLE TOM'S SAWMILL

CHARLES POTTS

The whine of the saw
Rips the heart.

We'll all die if we can't have
Old growth trees to cut
Slaves to drive
Our own way.

ESCAPE

LISA QUINLAN

Each afternoon, the sun catches her eye and leads her,
dreamlike, across a blown out field to a homestead cabin recently
abandoned by her only friends and the last of their neighbors. The tiny
cabin stands shadowed and safe in a grove of lovely trees.

The slim young woman steps slowly onto the shiny luxury of a
hardwood floor where yellow light from a west window floods her spot.
The room becomes a cabaret filled with loyal adoring fans.

She slips out of a faded print dress, folds it neatly and lays it in
a corner. Slender arms rise to loose flowing red hair down her back.
She stands, naked, motionless in the brilliant yellow sun, watches her
shadow on the floor, then begins to dance. Her giant shadow moves
with her, swaying and bending. Long fan-like fingers gracefully open
and then close again. Emotion and beauty fill the spotless cabin.

Her shadow fades as the sun slides lower. She dresses quietly
and carefully closes the cabin door. Her bare feet raise puffs of gray
dust as she walks away from the sun toward home.

He sits slouched, an empty jug of homemade beer at his feet,
dozing fitfully. He wonders, even in sleep, if the rain will come in time
to save the fragile, struggling wheat. Rough whiskers cover a tired and
wind burned face.

She wipes a paring knife on her dress and trims the skin from
a few small potatoes, slices them, and drops them into a greasy skillet.
She walks to a single rough opening carved into the side of the soddy
and watches a woodpecker bang his head against a tree made ghostly
by the last dying rays. She admires a breeze that conducts shadows in
a soft, perfect movement. A scorching smell demands her return.

The skillet clattering on the stove wakes her grunting mate. He
grumbles something about a burned dinner and slouches down again.

She looks at him with a used up sadness in her eyes, then
smiles, knowing tomorrow the sun will hold her again.

THE STEPCHILD

VESS QUINLAN

The muse visits me,
As she does all her children,
But I am stepchild.
She leaves her natural offspring
Exquisite poems, makes them gifts
Of words that fit together
Like the stones of ancient pyramids.
But I, the abused sibling,
Am treated differently.
She eats up all my oatmeal,
Lectures me on perseverance,
And refuses to return
Until I make fresh oatmeal.

COYOTES AND WATERMELONS

VESS QUINLAN

Some facts are great fun
Not useful, perhaps, or important
Except that they delight the mind.

Watermelon hearts are a coyote breakfast
Is a favorite minor fact
Because few people know it.
But I remember pre-dawn patrols
With grandfather and his shotgun,
To defend acres of ripe melons
From the crafty predators.

We would walk along straight rows
And count the hapless victims,
Step gingerly to avoid tender leaves
And scattered hunks of red flesh,
Note the incriminating paw prints
And vines ripped mercilessly from the earth.

I would offer to stay up
And guard the melon field;
Grandfather would say
I was too small for a shotgun.
I did not care for shooting;
I wanted to see
How a coyote opened a watermelon.

SAINT FRANCES 1951

VESS QUINLAN

Ten
And the morning saga
of Nancy Drew
Continues.

I put the spurs
To my old chair,
Book on lap,
And head south;
Narrow rubber tires
Seek traction
On the freshly waxed
Catholic clean floor.

The boss sister
Tries to head me
But I outrun her,
Skid through the door
Of 305
Expecting to see
Long red hair
And a bright smile
Over the ugly
Plastic lung
That provides breath.

There is only spotless
Linen stretched tight
And perfectly made
Triangle corners.
"Where is she?"
I ask.

The tough old nun,
Hands tightly clasped,
Face dissolving,
Looks away
And lies.

THE TROPHY

VESS QUINLAN

Each year he makes
His bed higher and deeper.
Instinct tells him solitude
And thick dark timber
Are his only choice.

Nearly twenty fat summers
On lush high country grasses
And as many brutal falls
Battling tawny young challengers
Has left him a sightless eye
And a stubborn stiffness
On these cold mountain mornings.

He rises, stretches carefully,
And stands quietly, listening,
As the rattling bugles
Of sons and grandsons
Echo across the valley.

The great gray bull
Lays heavy antlers
Carefully on his broad back,
Looks past his wide muzzle
With the one good eye
And walks slowly out
From the mothering spruce
Into a welcome bullet.

JOHN DEERE DREAMING

JIM TEX RATHS

John Deere dreaming—endless circles in the prairie dust
wishing I were somewhere else
The tractor roars its diesel song,
              the baler chunks and thunks along
Twelve plunger strokes, the knotter trips,
              another bale is born
Stroke and tie, stroke and tie
The baler machine symphony
John Deere dreaming—simple dreams,
              the noise destroys complex thought
Simple dreams like mountain streams,
              cool and clear shady there
Or Kristol—lovely Kristol in all her naughty nakedness
Now there is a thought for a thousand bales
And the tractor takes another round,
              another bale hits the ground
You and me by the lake and those lips, those lips
those luscious lips
Kristol, did I ever tell you I loved you most all of July
And the flywheel cranks and the knotter trips
And the sun climbs higher in the sky
Some January day—forty below—I'll chop these damned bales
in an arctic gale
And curse the cold and biting winds
              so far gone from heat and flies
But now it's twelve and tie, twelve and tie
John Deere dreaming on a hot summer day

THE BOX DINNER

BUCK RAMSEY

I

He topped his breakfast sopping bread
Through puddled syrup of sorghum,
And mulled his problem once again:
His church, it had no organ.

His parson missus hymned right in
And harmonized his worry,
"The Lord may hear the sparrow fall,
But he would have to hurry

"To catch the sound your whole flock makes
In congregation singing,
And still he'd think it jays and crows
Hard at their best mudslinging.

"Here's one thing: we're so far away
From any part of Heaven;
Two: count the choir and keys they're in,
The count would come out even."

His flock were few and well he knew
The money of the sinner
Would have to pay the organ's way.
And how? The old box dinner.

II

A bunch of the fellers were parked around posing
On pack crates and stave barrels and stacks of sack feed.
A few looked right towny and some wore the clothing
That pegged them as part of the cowpuncher breed.

The place was "The Public All Purpose Provider,"
But clearly its purpose for this motley crew
Was providing chambers deemed fit to consider
Each vital world issue that passed in review.

So Adams, the owner, was pleased passed the showing
When Bertrand St. Claire, the big spender walked in,
But he was let down when it came to the knowing
A dime for red ribbon was all he would spend.

"Red ribbon," mocked one waddie lolled on a pack crate,
"You aim to start braidin' and bowin' yer hair?"
"Not quite yet," said St. Claire. "This ribbon here should make
It certain I won't bid a box unaware."

The tribunal all latched as one to his meaning:
He bought the red ribbon to furnish to Miss
Fair Donner, the object of this season's preening
He trailed like some peacock with one ardent wish.

The red ribbon purchase was meant for the teacher
To tie her box dinner so St. Claire would know
Which box he should bid on to make sure he'd treat her
To his full attention—all this even though

The schoolmarm turned back all his ardent advances—
She knew he was known as the local Don Juan
Who charmed other ladies and teased all their fancies
And left each the sadder and left each alone.

She wrapped the red ribbon around her box dinner
And told him that he would know hers by its wraps.
But it was plumb tiny, for all she put in her
Wrapped box was an onion—a message, perhaps?

What neither knew, when he left, those scheming sinners
Concocted a ploy that would throw a big hitch
In St. Claire's big scheme, making sure many dinners
Were wrapped so that no one could know whose was which.

They bought plenty ribbon to furnish the women
They knew would pack boxes to win them the prize
Of a mate for a meal. So the tables were brimming
With red-ribboned boxes alike but in size.

A young man a greener could tell was a cowboy
Stood propping a wall on the spectator side,
And clutching a finger was his son, the one joy
Left to him when death took the mother, his bride.

Yes, Fiddle Tremain brought his kid to the auction,
Kid Tybo's first foray from the old Star Cross Ranch.
So Fiddle had range smarts, this fine son and gumption
But, short on the jingle, had hardly a chance

To buy a box dinner to share with a lady,
Though, lord knows, he showed up to be unalone.
But once when the bidding slacked off he thought maybe
One box could be bid on with little and won.

The package was tied with the same bright red ribbon
That most of the boxes were tied with that night,
But this one was near tenth their size, so not bid on
But by just one bidder. So all turned out right.

When he got a smile and a nod from Fair Donner,
St. Claire bid the biggest box near out of sight.
And, bidding completed, he "deemed it an honor"
To dine with the wife of the preacher that night.

The parson, weeks later, was proud of the organ-
Accompanied praise he could pay to his Boss.
But, all in all, surely by far the best bargain
Was sealed when Fair Donner moved to the Star Cross.

POEM NOTES

BUCK RAMSEY

When he was 92, George Hayden told me
As a young cowpuncher he roped a black bear
Close to where I live.
Back then it was out on the plain
The closest brush miles north in the river breaks.
Now it is a neighborhood
Of stylish town dwellings
Seven or eight to the block
A lush place for a prairie town
Though the only remnant ancient growth
Not lurking underground and waiting to emerge
If there is devastation and the bricks crumble
Are the wild flowers cultivated profusely
In the transplanted meadow
My wife has made of our front yard
A bouquet to keep me home
My conceit would sometimes have it
Though I'm smart enough to know
The statement of its creatrix
Is something far other and larger.

Yard judges passing out ribbons
Would not stop here
Would instead give the blue to the yard
Of a professional man who dons denim
And expensive leather lace-up boots weekends

To go out on the range where his basic
College courses in entomology and botany
Come in handy as he catalogues species
And compares their numbers with those
Documented from buffalo times.
People conscience laden with their place
Among things take on avocations like this.
He mails his lamentations
For lost bugs and shrubs
To a central computer in a brick building
Growing out of asphalt operated by folks
Who live on lots much like his
Where atavism lurks only in the willful cockroach
And doomed spider or sprig of native grass.

The red ribbon would go to the rancher
Who owns much of the range he walks weekends.
They live only blocks apart
And unaware share the same yard man.
The rancher's daddy was not good to the grass
And he isn't either but is getting better
For sometimes in his sleep
He dreams a look from an old puncher
Who has lived in a camp on his place
Since his daddy was a young man.
The look in the occasional dream
Is telling the rancher something
He is beginning to understand.
The old puncher got the attitude of the look

From an old cowpuncher who picked it up
From another mentor in the lineage
Who talked with old people
Who had been here all along.

The professional man with the avocation
Finds that he takes more notes
About things living and that lived before
While he visits the old cowpuncher in his camp
Than he takes on his long walks.

By chance one day
The man with the avocation and the rancher
Will meet in the cowpuncher's camp
Will go sit down by the river
And hear some resonance from the time
The sisters of the Creatrix
Sang the names of things
And they will talk about the New Millennium
In a language forgotten in this one
And guided by the old cowpuncher's look
And the attitude of the lineage
They will talk gladly and with good manners
Till that happy moon when things
Come clear and begin to fit together
In an olden way we will again remember.

THE TERRORIST

BUCK RAMSEY

If I were a poet, a prominent one
Who might at times be asked for interviews
I would be true to the usual type
And ready with answers, and if I were,
As surely I would be, asked a question
About what the function of poetry is
I would say, perhaps, dangerous things, say:

It remembers what has always been known,
Pierces all memory with what is felt
And celebrates it, and celebrates too
What is often found the first place one looks,
Pieces together the strange relations.

Another thing, such little sparks as these
Flying loose from pen and pencil frictions—
How shall I say?—palliate, so to speak,
The occasional urge for lighting bombs.

Consider what I might have been doing
Had I not been becoming this poet,
Had I not been, in anger at anguish,
Trying to horn through, maybe hoove over
The high hard slick wall the world roars behind
To drive home a point to the howling crowd.

Always again frustrated, again hurt
And stunned to silence, I want to bawl out,
Then the muse's billowing cape beckons
My mad bull glare again till, lured, I charge
Again for the insubstantial middle,
And with a bellowing choked back by a lump
I gore and gore around the empty air.

Ah, pray for you the muse keeps me busy
Enough at this till finally I am
Thrust cleanly down between the shoulder blades.

LONE STAR WOMAN

HANK REAL BIRD

Twas half moon out on the longest day
Twas rodeoin' about Oklahoma way
Walked in a feelin' late at night
Took me a chance turned out right
A Lone Star woman held me tight
She talked of love how it ought to be
Love in thought and just be free
That's what she said, said to me
Feelin' love and feelin' free
Feelin' free and feelin' love.

A Lone Star woman whispered love
Took it away before the dawn
A Lone Star woman in my mind
A Lone Star woman back in time
Dreamin' of a feelin', in a dream
A Lone Star woman back in time.

Drivin' down wind river
I'm rodeo bound, long road to hoe
With Lone Star woman on my mind
All I can do is think of her
Back in time when she was mine
She talked of love how to make love grow
You give a lot but not enough
That's the way to make love grow
Feelin's Flow and love will grow
Love'll grow when feelin's flow
Feelin's flow and love will grow

A Lone Star woman whispered love
Took it away before the dawn
A Lone Star woman in my mind
A Lone Star woman back in time
Dreamin' of a feelin', in a dream
A Lone Star woman back in time.
A Lone Star woman whispered love
Took it away before the dawn

DRIFTWOOD FEELIN'

HANK REAL BIRD

How much longer
Do you want
To be in the wind
Elk River's edge
There I am standin'
Lookin' for a feelin'
In the roar of the water
Come down river lookin' around
Feelin' gotta roam.

Driftwood feelin'
Floatin' down love river
Hearts way can't do
I'm catchin' a ride
Driftwood feelin'
Floatin' down love river
Hearts way can't do
I'm catchin' a ride
Floatin' down love river.

Somewhere
Between the reflection and the stars
Is the feelin' of life in love
Where you could hear
The stars in the wind
Feelin', twinklin', and flutterin'

In cottonwood leaves
Just a feelin' in the wind
In yesterday from days gone by
Can I have tomorrow
From yesterday, that I borrow?

Driftwood feelin'
Floatin' down love river
Hearts way can't do
I'm catchin' a ride
Driftwood feelin'
Floatin' down love river
Hearts way can't do
I'm catchin' a ride
Floatin' down love river.

GREEN LANTERN BAR/EL PASO, TEXAS

KELL ROBERTSON

Mamacita gives a plate of beans
to her retarded son and brings me
a glass of beer and counts
the two quarters twice before
punching fifty cents
on the antique register.
The barmaid, Karen, a gringa
from Kansas arrives with
another black eye and a plea
for enough money to bail him
out of jail again. She sits
next to me and looks through
my notebook. "You don't fool me,"
she says, "We're both hustlers.
I hustle for money and drugs—
you hustle for these words of yours."
Mamacita tells her it's time
to go to work. She hurries
into the back to put on eyeshadow
and smoke a joint and struts
back out looking like a sad
tarnished cheerleader. The
retarded son, beans dripping from
his chin, puts his hand on mine
and says
   "God bless you
      God bless me
         God bless Mama
            In the sea . . ."
It's about all he can say
and it's just about enough.

THE OLD MAN GOES HOME

KELL ROBERTSON

Under the discount store
the fast food place
the furniture outlet
under all that asphalt
is one of the best chunks
of black bottom farm land
in southeast Kansas.
My grandad grew corn
wheat, oats and alfalfa,
rotating the crops by
his almanac and the taste
of the dirt, and there
under that corner
my grandma's garden grew.
The house was somewhere
near the bicycle rack
and the barn was where
they have that bank
of video games.

Under all this asphalt and concrete
plastic and steel, I learned to cut
a calf, learned to drive a team of horses,
learned to work in this earth
and in that barn, learned
from a third cousin who

teetered on the edge of womanhood
another meaning for kisses
beyond the peck on the cheek
I got from grandma.

I close my eyes and see it,
butt my way under that old Jersey cow
squirt the hot steaming milk
into the cold tin bucket, hear
the hogs snorting around for slops
we saved for them.

I open my eyes and almost
get run over by a housewife
with a buggy full of disposable diapers
and sugar coated cereals.

The security guard takes my arm, asks
if I'm alright, leads me out into the parking lot
asks me what I'm doing there if I'm not
going to buy anything.

I'm visiting my grandad's farm I say
underneath all this crap
is the sweetest little farm
in southeast Kansas.

Walking away
into the shimmering heat
rising from the parking lot
I swear I hear
grandma calling us for supper.
There'll be beans and cornbread
and iced tea . . . tomorrow we'll start
plowing the lower forty.
Then we'll come home and sit
on the front porch, watching the dogs
playing in the yard, dreaming
of going to town next week
to sell some hay and get
a store bought hat
to wear at the dance at the Grange Hall.
Maybe my cousin will be there
and she'll teach me more
about this kissing business.

Right now
looking back at the parking lot
full of people doing something

all I can see is what we've lost.

farmers still

ANNE SLADE

at the kitchen table
we cup our hands around coffee mugs
to fight off the chill of fall rains
we talk about late harvest and sprouting swaths
and the whims of marketing boards money-lenders
and mother nature

we remember past years with bumper crops
and how the north-east quarter always produces
but this year the swaths are under water
and tough as things seem it's not so bad as Harrison's
after their auction last year they moved to the city

they say they used to lie awake wondering if the old boss cow
made it through the winter if the brockle-faced heifer
calved on her own
they drive out to check other people's crops on land
their grandfather homesteaded
stop in at coffee row   talk about the weather
like they were still here

lawrence

ANNE SLADE

lawrence lives down the valley
he was born there some eighty years ago
tells us he'd never live anywhere else
not that he hasn't traveled
but he's got everything he needs on that home quarter
his cows and garden and memories

lawrence recalls times we never hear about in history books
like how when he was young the indians camped along willow creek
and taught him everything he knows about fishing
lawrence learned to reach under the riverbank
where the trout rested deep in the shadows
he'd lie silently his fingers floating in the water
till the fish wriggled close
then lawrence would squeeze that trout and
toss it onto the riverbank

he swears all you ever need in life is patience
and the right place to wait

LOVE AND WAR

Myrt Wallis

For my Sons
and for Rod and Bill
sons of my heart

Young Crow warriors rode into war
their hearts filled with joy
Wanting to live with courage and honor
Willing and eager to die for glory

Raised in danger, deprivation and love
Taught what to do when
The fear and the pain came
Sent up the mountain alone
Fasting and freezing
Flesh-pierced and dancing
Sun-parched and thirsting
Misery and terror brought visions
Giving direction to life

Knowing their enemy, they flew
Straight into battle
Loving their enemy, they dashed
Forward to count coup
And become men.

My sons, reluctant warriors, sent into war
Sorrow filling their hearts
Wanting to live with courage and honor
Willing, not eager, to die for duty

Raised in comfort and safety and love
Sunday school taught to
Love thy neighbor, all are equal
Turn the other cheek, cooperate
Wear your overshoes
Be careful when crossing the street
Then tried to teach you to hate
An unknown enemy enough
To kill him.

I wish you could let go
of the sorrow and guilt
I pray you will give up
The pain of remembering
It wasn't your fault.
We didn't raise you right.

GIRLFRIENDS

SUE WALLIS

In our twenties
To celebrate
We whipped men at pool
Drove a hundred miles
To a country dance
On five dollars
Easy

Now we rejoice
In faded flannel nighties
Chocolates, a bottle of wine
And old Tarzan movies
Giggling about wild times
And those men

Six horse hitches
Bound for gay old dances
Couldn't drag us
Off these couches
De-afghan us

Handsome fellers
Lined up asking
Couldn't tempt us
From this pleasure

It's too precious
It's too rare
That's why we call it

Our Indulgence

GRANDPA LEW

Sue Wallis

glassed an eye that wasn't there
barn buckin' bronc
and a piece of rafter wood
left sorry sight.

shaved his head
talked crude and didn't care
called biscuits dummies
called shit, shit.

shod horses at sixty-eight
was hard and rough
on stock and kids and wives
but never drank.

died old and tough and deaf
his good eye bad
they buried him in ashes
two in a one man plot.

doesn't care
that they went such lengths
to put him with three generations
of a dead fam'ly.

doesn't care
that the second worn-out wife
will eventually share
his singular slot.

remains as lonely as life
remembered as
ornery.

BUNCH QUITTER

SUE WALLIS

She is a proud half-brahma mama in the middle of a mindless herd
Where she knows she don't belong

She'll throw her high-horned head and test the air
Circle quick (and bawl) to tuck that baby in her flank
Then break and run high-tailed
Up every steep and narrow, brushy side draw
She can find.

So if you're gonna think to stop her
You'll have to see the signs
And you better be there—
Mounted
Before she ever sniffs the wind

Like me she has a spiritual affinity for solitude
For lotsa grass and running creeks and growing babies by her side
She seeks the serene protection of Alone—
The security of Wild Empty

And though I know she sometimes longs
For the complacency of bunching
Like I sometimes yearn
And revel
In the intimate connections
Of humanity

Still, like me, she knows deep down inside
That herds of any kind are dangerous
And far too unreliable
For trust.

COYOTE BITCH

SUE WALLIS

Tonight . . .

I feel like a Coyote Bitch
(in heat)
Do not annoy me, tempt me, or toy with me
I have been lonely too long

An old bitch will wait with native intellect
Run just below the ridges
You won't see her 'til she catches
That first waft of
Rottenness

She'll linger ruthless
Over the carrion carcass
Of some uncaring
Wild Steer

Then drag the stinking skin
Back to her solitary den
To chew and slobber and maul the hide
Long after all hint of flesh is dried

Just for comfort
Mangling idle dreams of regal wolfish lovers
Strong and smart and beautiful

. . . Who never appear

SADDLIN'-UP TIME

ANDY WILKINSON

I never looked forward to the end of the day,
Or to evening, drab and melancholy-gray,
Or to featureless shadows of purple-to-black,
Or to work finished-up or simply put back
While the business of living slowly unwinds;
I was always awaitin' for saddlin'-up time.

I slept of necessity, not pleasure, and not
For the comforts of night, when the bosom of God
Cradled mortality in immortal dark,
Nor for the shroud of cool starlight whose spark
Like the lamp of the firefly silently chimed;
I took my pleasure in saddlin'-up time.

And I worried the hectic commotion of morn,
The commerce of mercantile and courthouse lawn,
The meetings and greetings on sidewalk and street
Where horseback-opinions and auguring meet,
And I argued their rhythms, swore at their rhymes,
But was playful as a pup, come saddlin'-up time.

For 'twas then before ever light angled to fill
The round corners, we'd clamor like wolves at the kill
With horse-talk our yap, with our nip and our bite
Latigo leathers snapping cinches down tight
In the summer's wet dew or the winter's sharp rime
As we readied our horses at saddlin'-up time,

When the morning night air was marble we breathed,
Heavy and smooth and as cold as the breeze

That skitters across the new snow-covered plains,
One hand on the horn and the other, the reins
We stepped aboard stirrups, young bucks in our prime,
Salty as the Pecos at saddlin'-up time.

Though I've lived for this moment most all of my life,
Beginnings, not endings, put the edge on my knife;
I've cursed too damn much and I've never prayed well
And it may be God figures to send me to Hell,
Riding drag for the Devil to pay for my crimes,
But I'm damned if I'll go 'fore saddlin'-up time.

HORSEBACK ON THE LLANO ESTACADO

ANDY WILKINSON

The wind is the oldest river, rhythmic,
Unceasing, infinite, the pulse of God.
Where time is the blood in which the Llano
Is washed, where the horizon is the line
Cut from forever by the eddies
Of this current, spinning and swirling
On the nether edge of sight, patient as starlight,
There we ride like Coronado, his breath
At our backs and our eyes screwed to his dreams
Of shining cities floating over the prairie.
There, like Quanah Parker, we are waves
On this river, riding ponies like fishes,
Sleek, quick, nimble. And, like Goodnight,
There we ride with the wind in our faces
Until we find its roots, until the last
Gust lies stilled and settled on the fences,
Until the wind is a river no more.

F.M. 168, BUFFALO LAKE TO NAZARETH

ANDY WILKINSON

This road lay like an invitation, south
From the commercial highway, straight into
The Llano Estacado's rolling gut

Where tides of grass rose and fell in pastel
Yellow swells beneath a blue beyond which
There was no cause for sky, where taut fences

With steel goat-head barbs and stout cedar posts
Kept cattle in communion, tractors out
And left the wind to wander at her will.

The sweet insinuation of this road
Was a highway cafe waitress winking
As she licked her pencil lead and asked me

What I wanted, was a rodeo queen
With a quirt in her teeth, a barrel horse
Between her legs and her saddle-slick jeans

Smoother than sweet cream, was an angel wing
Lost in the sun but circling shadows down
To the center stripe as mercy given.

Like a superstition, this road prickled
The hair on the back of my neck, made me

Sit up straight in the seat of my old van,

Made me crank the windows down and snap
The radio off, made me hold the wheel
Light like reins and let the Chevrolet

Have her head and roll like she and this road
Knew one another well in that life
Where journey and destination were the same.

AT THE GRAVE OF BILLY THE KID

ANDY WILKINSON

I stopped at the grave of Billy the Kid.
He was a man that needed killing, not
A museum and a gift-and-curio shop

Where knick-knacks and trinkets and souvenirs
Argue for attention with his archived death
Certificate. Out back, enshrined in cyclone fence

To keep the gawking worshipers at bay,
Rest his remains. As live *touristas*
Well-outnumbered dead *pistoleros* today,

I stayed in the car, saved the admission fee,
And drove west past awkward softball diamonds
And concrete picnic tables toward the river

To the remains of the fort where Billy
Was shot dead in a house that was once
The quarters of the officers who led the men

Who kept the Apache and the Navajo
In the concentration camp at Bosque Redondo
At the end of the Long Walk. Hunger

And disease and soldiers and busted hearts
Killed three thousand old and young, women
And men, babies and children. Perhaps there were

Outlaws among them, too; I just don't know,
Because there were no death certificates,
No shrines, no graves on display. When I left,

Headed east down Highway Sixty, I saw
Jet fighters carving low and sweeping
Arcs on imaginary bombing runs

Over the Melrose Range, and I remembered
Last night, in Santa Fe, the bright moon, full
And round as the circle that moves the world.

THE PEOPLE FROM THE VALLEY
—for Frank Waters

KEITH WILSON

The farmers come, come
on down the Pecos Valley
in busted-bottom wagons

their children thin
blonde cornhusk hair
blowing

Sparrows watch dry ruts
for spilled kernels
the men, stiff, formal

black suits, white shirts,
the women searching for
other wagons, bright bonnets

Cottonwood leaves clash
green in Saturday's wind
as the quiet children sit

aware they will be watched by
townboys in their victor clothes,
the dark eyes of townsmen

watching for any beauty
the land has missed, its
women, this land hungers

for women, and for farmers
who can write their own obituaries
in the lines of their hard hands.

PORTRAIT OF A FATHER

KEITH WILSON

My father was a hard man, closed
off from what he could not understand.
One night he tried to pry off the ring
from my mother's hand, she in a coma,

he with a new woman waiting for the bright
glimpse of diamond in the darkened room—
it flashed and mother sighed, moved
as he slipped back through the door.

He walked tall, had big hands, quick
smile—"Could charm the ears off a mule,"
his brother said, knowing him too well.
I remember the smell of smoke and cedar.

Men would follow him anywhere, it was said
they covered for him when he disappeared
into alcoholic odysseys along the Mexican Border,
whores and drunken fights two weeks long.

I remember him smelling of vomit and urine,
barely alive for days, then him striding out
his big shoulders straight, blue eyes
with diamond glints in the hard sun.

Surrounded by dust, roar of Caterpillar
engines, waving his hands, conducting work
into a symphony of labor and the rough road
emerged from violated land, was polished to

smooth asphalt right down to the thin white
stripe that ran on to forever. My father,
moving on, saying little, his green felt hat
scrunched down over his eyes, bent slightly

as if he walked against a stiff wind, the world
always at his back, neck muscles tensed, expectant,
a fighting man Snort Woods said "who couldn't tell
an enemy from a friend, what was his from what was not."

I remember the dust of the desert, the smell
of engine oil. The way his hands held a coyote pup
and how he laughed as the pup struck out, the white
flashing teeth flickering like gems in the dry air.

DESERT CENOTE

KEITH WILSON

There is sadness among the stones
today, the rabbits are silent.

No wind. The heat bears down.
It has not rained for one year.

We have faith out here, desert
people, we wait, knowing with sureness

the swift cross of clouds, the blessings
of moisture (to deprive a man is to give

charms to him). I love this dry land
am caught even by blowing sand, reaches

of hot winds. I am not the desert
but its name is not so far from mine.

Cenote is Spanish-Aztec for "waterhole, oasis"

SPRING—*for Rudy Anaya*

KEITH WILSON

All night he could hear the noise.
In the morning, the plains lay
like pages of sunlight, no wind.
He hurried past the village,
through the Breaks, saw the crest
come down, heaving, adobe earth,
carrying uprooted trees, parts
of wooden houses from upstream.

The Rio Pecos had gone crazy again.
Rio Loco, the old man had called it once.
Quicksand in the Summer, floods in the Spring,
dry as hell in Winter. Rio Loco.
Ought to build a dam, the old man said.
Stop that crazy river in its tracks.
Now he could see what Old Tom meant.
A heavy snake gutting the Valley.

A young girl in a pinafore, pale
silk hair spun by him, her arms out
stretched, blue eyes open, was gone
before his muscles could even tense,
whirled away, turning and turning
into the dark water and he knew
through his trembling that this
was the first Spring he had ever known
with some kind of truth and backed up
quickly as the River ate the land
from under his feet, passed him by.

COW DOGS

KEITH WILSON

The ranches I knew as a boy—
it was the Depression then,
though as my father used to say,
it's all we've ever known,
Depression, but we do all right.

Skinny steers and no market,
ranchers doing the work
because they've always done it,
waiting, nursing Durham butts,
cursing the lack of rain.

Even the dogs were thin
in those years. Dogs were part
of a ranch, guarding, yelping,
chasing chickens for sport
when nobody was looking, cocky

plumetailed dogs who looked like
fourlegged cowpunchers, took
the same airs, the same lazy tension
as they waited for action, any kind
of excitement. One old dog I remember

used to be able to throw a young calf
without hurting him much. In the evenings
the hands would gather and he would
rise slowly, carefully, walk to the corral
catch the calf running and throw him

neat as the devil into a cloud of early
evening dust. "It wasn't much," Old Jonesy
used to say, "but it sure as Hell
took your mind off your problems."

Dust rising from the baked earth,
night settling on the silent ranch.

FLEETING MOMENTS

Bill Wood

A quarter-mile from the ranch house
Lookin' off toward ol' Sand Creek
A'top a high divide
A lonely rider gazes out
At a stretch of open prairie
Where two brothers built a homestead
And he spots two forms a'comin'
Through the sagebrush to the South.

An ol' horse 'n' his young rider
And a single open heifer
Yet unwilling to be driven
Tries to dodge to no avail.
The heart inside the watchman
Keepin' vigil from afar
Leaps with joy at their successes
'Gainst just one of life's travails.

With intense determination
As is most the time with cow brutes
She runs and turns back harder
To evade her youthful foe.
Not all teachers, though, are human
And the cow-wise equine veteran
Shows his child pupil
Where to be and how to go.

Then with one last futile gesture
The heifer sulls into submission
Whereupon this youthful cowhand
Chuckles to himself with pride.
Pats 'n' praises his old cowhorse
Then points this critter northward
While she ambles ever slowly
'Till she's locked up safe inside.

Then the rider on the ridgetop
Slips way, yet undetected,
With emotion swelling inward
The kind that some men just don't share.
He well knows this moment's fleeting
Never to be recreated
All the costs to come well worth it.
That a father's forced to bear.

For the day is swift approaching
When the child will be leaving
Will he come back, will he stay?
Only God almighty knows.
If it is that he so chooses,
To come back to those beginnings,
Then his father will be waiting——
But that's not always how it goes.

A quarter-mile from the ranch house
Lookin' off toward ol' Sand Creek
A 'top a high divide
A lonely rider gazes out
At a stretch of open prairie
Where two brothers built a homestead
His aging eyes are searching
Through the sagebrush to the South . . .

THE FOUR HORSE HITCH

JERRY WRIGHT

As the Monsignor stampedes through
the wedding mass in "nine-o," record time—
we three cowpuncher heathens,
Copenhagen taut lips in our pews,
give silent thanks to the priest's pity.
Loosening collars and mopping brow sweat,
we blame the August prairie heat
and cinched up neck ties for our discomfort—
none willing to admit to ourselves
or another, the inevitable.
The lone remnant member
of the four horse hitch,
is now in the traces of another's rig.

Three colts and a filly,
coupled together from working age—
pulling each the other's burdens,
compensating for the other's lamenesses.

A mutual dependence and trust,
withstanding trials of years in the harness.
Outlasting bronc busted dreams,
cold jawed runaways,
and *Jack Daniels Black*.
Enduring our 14 karat gold filigreed visions,
religious conversions,
and bucket roping contests—
"just who's the saltiest with a *Coors* can
clenched tight in the teeth,
guzzling as the twine is twirled?"

Countless times I've watched,
separate auctions of matched teams—
never reckoning them unjust.
Though at this moment,
I feel their forlorn nickers,
panicked shrieks of separation haunt my mind.

With tall topped *Noconas*
slapping leather on sawdust in the Legion Hall,
I'm relieved the LeDoux is blaring loud—
drowning out my shattered heartbeats,
my pulse, galloping rimrock hoofbeats.
Dim Lights and a black *Resistoll* pulled low
cause shadows to disguise the flood
of memories as they well in my eyes.
My expression radiates best wishes
for the newlyweds—
But my soul aches for the days
of the four horse hitch,
and summers on Diamond Creek.

ZARZYSKI STOMACHS THE OXFORD SPECIAL WITH ZIMMER AT THE OX BAR & GRILL

PAUL ZARZYSKI

Donning his bronc-stomper black hat, cock-eyed
the morning after reading range rhymes
in Montana, Zimmer swears out loud
his belly's tough as whang leather,
reckons his grease count's a skosh low,
and it behooves us, here in cattleland,
to brunch on cow—no quiche,
no veggie omelet or henfruit Benedict
when Zimmer's craving beeve, a hoof-'n'-horn
dogie-puncher dose of B-12
to prod toward procreation
two braincells the whiskey failed to pickle.

Zarzyski thinks Zimmer figures
rare steak and eggs a pair
till he catches Zimmer's eyes, ruminating
behind the stained menu—that devious gleam.
Zimmer has brains on the mind.

Zimmer has brains on his mind
and Zarzyski knows too well The Zimmer Dictum:
what suits one P.Z., damned straight tickles
another P.Z. plum pink. Sure as shit
and shootin', like a gunslinger
demanding redeye, crusty-throated Zimmer hollers
"Bring us hombres brains and eggs."
And the waitress relays Zimmer's whimsy
to a fry-cook big enough to eat hay
and dirty-up the floor. In short-order lingo
she yells, "these boys **need 'em**, Sam—
these Z-boys **need 'em** real awful bad."

FLAMENCA DUENDE

PAUL ZARZYSKI

The duende is a power, not a work; it is
a struggle, not a thought . . . not a question
of ability, but of true, living style, of blood,
of the most ancient culture, of spontaneous
creation. . . . It is, in sum, the spirit of the earth.
—Federico Garcia Lorca

Not just any hot Latin blood, but the fiery
blood of Maria Benitez—her heart's
whole voltage into each muscle, perfect
choreography of the body's troupe,
500 strong—is not just any passion
but passion ahorseback
full-gallop with gut-stringed, cyprus guitars
to the stampede of hand clap, castanets,
laughter and tragic Andalusian wail
cracking the night like lightning
striking Gypsy moons afire.

Into this flamenca's dance goes the faith
of all saints, one poet's soul, vaquero savvy
and toreador grit, predator
frenzy at the taste of blood, plus a shot
of erotica, rage, and mother love.
When the blur of feet mesmerizes me—
holds me in the black bonds between stars—
I miss the gait of her eyes,

and when I follow her face, chin poised
for passage into the meteor storm of rhythms,
I miss the aerial steps of one hand. Yet,
when I focus on that flight,
the mate solos out of the frame—
impossible to track a duet
of acrobatic toucans through a tropical
canopy's kaleidoscopic dance.

But the Spanish, heir to that grace,
cheer her on: Olé! Maria! Olé!
and the ruffed grouse drumming
accelerates to cicada chirr, that chain
reaction of ricochets
rippling through the train of her gown,
through her shawl's foot-long fringes
flailing wild as hot wires
in a gale. As she pivots
finger-snap fast, an earring
whiplashed to the stage
flickers to life, ignited
by the charge of its atoms dancing—
dancing to the pulse of passion's lithe flame
burning for Maria
from the molten center of the earth—dancing,
that gold earring dancing till it too burns.

MARIA BENITEZ

PAUL ZARZYSKI

A bucking horse-twisting Gypsy
Trailing the moon to each show
I'm drawn to Maria's arena
In the piñons of New Mexico

Her castanets, they telegraph passion
Her Spanish heels are a Gatling gun quick
Like the fast ratchet sound of my rowels spinning 'round
And the ricochet ring when they click

> Víva Maria Benítez
> Olé Maria Olé
> Tú Estampa Flamenca
> Mi alma tan bronca
> Like a stampede through ol' Santa Fe
> Olé Maria Olé

Flamenco, Gitano, the Gypsy
The stage is her own Loving Trail
She's cool as a matador (dancing)
To a high Andalucian wail

And I ride on the wind of her rhythm
With her dance in my veins I can't lose
And I crave the bronc's fury and fire
The wild flame that we can't refuse

Víva Maria Benítez
  Olé Maria Olé
Tú Estampa Flamenca
Mi alma tan bronca
  Like a stampede through ol' Santa Fe
  Olé Maria Olé

I'll ride with her soul for 8 seconds
Each muscle a'rippling like hers
And I'll sing to her hoof-pounding tempo
This lovesong that trills from my spurs

  Víva Maria Benítez
    Olé Maria Olé
  Tú Estampa Flamenca
  Mi alma tan bronca
  Like a stampede through ol' Santa Fe
    Olé Maria Olé
      Víva Maria Olé

Maria Benitez was written as the lyric/song version of
Flamenca Duende in collaboration with John Hollis.

TO WALLACE

PAUL ZARZYSKI

I'm not applauding cathouse towns in Idaho,
nor rednecked gov'nors who reigned in Alabama.
The Wallace *I'm* yippee-ti-hurrayin' is my hero,
that Cowboy Poet Lariat—McRae,
from the Rocker Six, up Rosebud crick, Montana.

I said "Cowboy Poet," and those are two big words,
as tall and deep to fill as red-topped Paul Bond boots.
A Cowboy Poet cuts strong verses from the herds,
savvies cattle, horseflesh, grass, and water,
lives the history and tradition, loves their deepest roots.

And that fits Wallace, like his saddle, stem to stern—
land-loving navyman, cavvyman, pistolero poet.
And top-hand actor, too, they say, because he'll burn
and go for broke on that cowpoke hole card, heart—
Wallace packs the ace and he's damn proud to show it.

Which is why his five-gaited iambs move so true
with keen vision, image, spry rhythm, rhyme and wit.
The wise, old farrier hammering out a shoe—
Wallace loves that ballpeen-anvil chime
as he forges and he shapes each red-hot line to fit.

And how his flinty, roughstock eye can size-up folks—
between the slats, they earn his praise or wrath in verse.
From dancehall damsels to itinerant cowpokes,
his gavel's not as fast as Judge Roy Bean's,
but hanging from his gallows, made of words, is worse.

And hard—oh Lord—how he fought hard to save the land
from the greed-monger Kid Russell called "the booster."
When they demanded coal, he showed the bastards sand—
the grit of Sitting Bull and Crazy Horse
and Gallo de Cielo, Tyson's fighting rooster.

Did he win? Let's just say he doesn't know defeat—
there lives within the words, themselves, intrinsic worth.
You bet your kack, his verse will last beyond the beat
and power of those generating plants—
a poem-ghost-rider-posse crusading for the earth.

Cheers to Wallace! I'm proud to call my hero "Friend."
Long may the lingo of his calling ricochet and ring.
Montana's Champeen Bard hard-charging that front end
like Casey on a bronc, Wallace spurs the words
'cross puncher poetry arenas where he'll always be The King.